HOW TO ATTRACT THE RIGHT WOMAN

COMPREHENSIVE GUIDE TO GETTING THE WOMAN
A MAN NEEDS, AND TIPS ON HOW TO MAKE HER
FALL IN LOVE WITH YOU AND HAVE THE BEST
COUPLE RELATIONSHIP POSSIBLE.

By A. Gabriel Press

Contents

PROLOGUE

"I know that I know nothing."

-Socrates

Based on people's experiences, research, and personal points of view, this book is about how honestly a man can start a relationship and how that relationship can have a successful ending developing both man and woman as a couple and individually.

Without declaring infallibility, much less perfection of wise knowledge, but rather just authentic experience and honest observation, this book reflects the appropriate ways for a man to behave with a woman to conquer her affections.

Stated that everyone is different, or everyone is in a world of their own. Speaking about individuals' human character and personality is a serious and delicate matter.

As a result of mentioning all this, it is advisable to share a point of view with the hope that someone else may benefit from the experience of others. Moreover, reaffirming the knowledge or perhaps learning and getting to know something personally still ignored, others would want to share information with friends or loved ones to understand the relationship between men and women better.

Most people already know or have heard about man and woman relationships through books, television documentaries, discussions, etc., with experts in the social and the psychology of couple relationships.

Though is also true that sometimes when we think we already know it all, there are also things that we may have just not considered already.

Looking into the life experience of someone who has lived, suffered, been glad, been fortunate, and even been regretful when some things didn't end the desired way. The reasons for a failed relationship could be many and diverse in the pursuit of happiness with the right partner.

When we assume things, we may still be wrong because too much confidence may lead us to err. But on the other hand, practical contact and observation lead us to experiences that we can count on. That's why books have been so relevant through time because if we show serious interest in them, we can learn from the errors or successes of others and this way saving us lots of trouble.

His honorability, excellent physical appearance, and references attract a woman to a man more commonly. But, although it may not seem like it, she can also be interested in his origins and past, which can help build trust, the latter being what will define if he is a good catch.

Finding a sentimental partner is a vital task. However, sometimes you can think that there is no longer any candidate available and perhaps the last one has already been taken and there are no options left. That is when you must face the problem with a lot of creativity and intelligence.

When trying to please a woman is a good idea to think about the things she may need and see if the man in question is able or has the resources necessary to assure her positive response, which is vital for succeeding in trying to conquer her love.

A question that men have always asked themselves is.

What do women want? Until now, the research has tried to solve the mysteries of female behavior with some results that offer clues that clarify the old question a bit.

The point is that being the perfect man is not easy as it requires that both parties give a little of themselves to achieve a balance.

Having said this.

What are some of the elements required to be a woman's, ideal man?

We could say that the perfect man knows how to keep his wife happy; if someone achieves this goal, we can say he is the ideal man.

When a man is honest, a woman can trust him, and for a woman, honesty is desirable because it allows a relationship to deepen.

A good relationship rests on fundamental qualities, especially those that will not wane or diminish over time.

Among these are moral values such as honesty.

Since women, like men, all have different personalities and tastes, it cannot be generalized when stating what a woman looks for in a man. Still, we can consider the qualities women most commonly look for in a man.

So hopefully, the information here may help any reader who wishes to know about the requirements of the chosen significant other in the genuine pursuit of a happy relationship

PHYSICAL APPEARANCE

Any man may be in good spirits and good temper when he's well dressed. There isn't much credit in that.
– Charles Dickens

In searching for the best way to appear attractive to a woman, a man should consider that what may seem like a pretty appearance for some women may not be for another.

When considering the kind of woman, one tries to impress, it is best not to neglect to be consistent with oneself.

That way, someone can ensure is trying to please the right woman.

Therefore, the dressing should also be accordingly to who you are.

To create an authentic connection requires, first, dressing for yourself and allowing your personality to shine through. This way, people can better perceive your character.

Usually, people acquire and surround themselves with things that have to do with their personality, and clothing is one of those things.

Therefore, when dressing, it is advisable to wear your style, which will drive away the wrong people but attract the right woman or people.

Wearing clothes that make you feel comfortable with yourself will create the feeling of comfort and security that you need to attract the right woman or the right kind of people to you.

But what are the right factors we can call the correct appearance concerning the opposite sex besides clothing?

We could say that they are the physical characteristics we first notice in a person. And those characteristics are what will determine whether we like a person, for example, a person's hair, clothes, nose, age, and general appearance.

However, to talk about what a woman looks for in a man can be an extensive and complex matter; however, it shouldn't have to be so. So, let's get to the point, the vital and positive that matters the most.

A saying declares, "Love is born from sight" Therefore, the first impression is always the one that lasts.

Often the first judged aspect of a person is the physical appearance. And from there emerges an association with the intelligence, customs, and integrity of such person.

So, the hair also speaks of an individual's personality, and for a woman, a man's hair can influence whether she likes someone.

Although it is not a rule, some women will be more attracted to a slender man with a youthful appearance regardless of age. Also, if the man is taller than her, it will work in his favor, and finally, the masculine features of the face will have a notable influence.

Women prefer a man with a great personality and a kind heart, although the first visual impression attracts them the most.

Regardless of the current physical appearance of a guy, it is very advisable to consider the following features and even work on them as possible since these are the features most women look for in a man.

Height.

Some women will not deny their attraction to tall men and will even be proud to have a tall partner.

Eyes.

Some say that the eyes are the soul's windows and beautiful eyes speak for themselves, especially when trying to impress a woman.

Hair.

A clean and silky hair says a lot to a woman, although a good cut also counts.

Clothes.

An elegantly dressed man will always stand out from the rest, especially if a woman notices it.

The smile.

A man who smiles already has an advantage that will bring him closer to his favorite woman.

Hygiene.

Something of vital importance that easily attracts women is a well-groomed guy, and they will notice if a said man also uses perfume, something that a woman does not easily forget.

Also, something that attracts women and reveals someone who takes good care of his body is a physically fit man, highlighted by great six-pack abs, pecs, shoulders, forearms, and back.

It is no surprise that women prefer a man with well-defined muscles because they are a vital sign of masculinity.

However, it is necessary to mention that not all women feel attracted to fit, strong men because, for some women, other qualities are more critical.

Intelligence.

Although Intelligence is a factor that may be out of a total control, it is nonetheless something you can work on towards your success. Among some other favorable characteristics, consider an excellent physical posture. I once heard someone say in the form of advice. Walk like a king. And it's something I've never heard before, and it was uplifting and inspiring to listen to that.

Be optimistic with her, passionate, fun, have a good mood, and have a good spirit.

Many factors can define a man, and some of these factors belong to personality. Women always appreciate a man who takes risks, which is also vital in life in general.

That is why women avoid men who doubt and prefer men who are firm in their convictions.

It is notable that based on experience, there are women who are not necessarily attracted to physically attractive men because there are men who, despite lack of physical attractiveness, are friendly, fun, and master a wide range of topics when talking. Yet somehow women feel attracted to someone who says what he thinks and expresses it in pleasant ways.

Also, according to researchers of the behavior between the sexes, it is not necessarily true that only the physical element attracts the opposite sex.

Nevertheless, if a man wishes, he can transform his physical appearance through exercise as far as possible to look more exciting and attractive to girls, since it is in the genes to constantly seek solutions to any obstacles.

In searching for the attributes to please a woman, men must also consider the qualities that have nothing to do with a good physique. Yet also other qualities that women also look for in a man. Fortunately, not all women necessarily feel attracted to the stereotypes of the tall, dark-skinned, muscular man that many men think women are pursuing.

So, let's consider some other characteristics that men must possess to attract the desired woman.

Sometimes, when women look for a lasting relationship, they consider a man's availability paramount. So usually, they will be interested in whether a said man is married or single instead of pondering if he is a handsome and well-built guy.

Although it may seem illogical sometimes, we find couples that may seem unequal to each other. Still, in exchange for an excellent physical appearance, some partner couples can have things in common in their goals of a more stable and practical relationship.

Another fact is that some women would prefer a man's kindness and chivalry rather than choosing a playboy for a serious relationship.

Although it is also true that there are women who have no problem with a one-night stand. So, some women would prefer appearance instead of chivalry.

Some other characteristics to consider that attract women can be age. So, a man should not worry so much about age because studies in this regard have found that there are women who prefer their partner to be older than them. The supposed economic independence of a mature man can influence this behavior.

Humor also counts. Good humor in a man is an essential quality of personality that attracts women.

Experience and research demonstrate that optimism and laughter are a lovely combination. And laughter and happy moments are a solid foundation for a lasting relationship.

How about a pet?

Another way to appear familiar to a woman can be to own a pet, which can increase the chances of striking up a conversation with a girl because it is unlikely that a girl doesn't like a puppy. We could say that even in a situation like making friends with a girl, a dog is still a man's best friend.

Also, something worth considering is showing interest in her goals, expectations, and dreams, even showing that you have an interest in her closest relatives.

And once she already has familiarity with you, try to keep continuous interest in her everyday life, which is something that will tell her she is important to you.

Finally, take risks. There is nothing to lose and much to gain, and sometimes the simplest thing is the right thing. Many men lose opportunities due to insecurities, and if they don't dare approach a girl, they will never know if she would have reciprocated. Often a man's first instinct is the right one, so act, and you will gain invaluable experience for yourself. Besides, you don't know if she may be expecting you to be brave enough to give the first step. So be of good cheer. And good luck.

BEING THE RIGHT MAN FOR HER

You'd be surprised how fast things happen when the right man comes along

– Danielle Steel

Even though looks may help with a first impression, an essential thing in a relationship is how your partner supports you and brings you joy. Simply looking at physical attributes is a shallow mindset, and one should broaden their view on appearance by getting to know someone regardless of how they look.

A man can also appear attractive to a woman if he is compassionate, caring, and loving. Those qualities could make a good father or lifelong companion, so these too define the qualities of a great attractive man.

Smile.

Another quality that most women like in a man is a sense of humor because a good laugh always eases the tension making any moment a great moment to feel good.

Faithfulness.

Fidelity is something innate that any woman wants in a man, and if a man possesses the character of being faithful, he is likely to have a happy woman.

The right man for a woman is the one who knows how to respect and trust her. But unfortunately, there is no better option or one that guarantees respect and a good understanding in a man-woman relationship than fidelity.

Loyalty is not something that can be bought or expected from someone if the requirements of respect and trust are not present. However, we can expect fidelity from a woman if we work hard to save and protect our relationship with her.

Trustworthy.

We cannot learn to be trustworthy

like other qualities that a person could possess but being trustworthy is something that we can only instill in somebody. Above all, being a reliable person is like a lifestyle. Being loyal is something that has to do with character.

Think correctly, using common sense, and seeking mutual goodness in each other is a necessary quality that attracts anyone, especially women. People who possess this quality obtain a good reputation and respect in dealing with people. In the couple's sphere, this quality is of great esteem for a woman.

Therefore, if a man possesses this quality, he will become a successful man in his pursuit of the love of a woman.

Drive and purpose.

Obtaining the love of a woman is a reasonable goal.

However, it will most likely be necessary for a man to have other objectives that will complement and ensure the complete success of the primary goal.

Besides, there is nothing as exciting and attractive as a man who has other goals in life.

So, a male should have other different objectives besides those of the relationship, which will help the couple make life more enjoyable, lasting, and more secure, especially financially.

Therefore, if both have the desired love and own goals, that will create the appropriate environment to develop the potential for a happy and prosperous relationship.

It will be ideal if a couple meets these characteristics. And if it is only the male who has this aptitude, the relationship can also be successful. However, the latter will be essential if it is only the man who has the resources to withstand unexpected issues.

In the world, there are successful women, but if the man they have chosen is not like them. Then, the relationship is likely to lack credibility, which will make the ties unstable, unfortunately.

Although in life, there are always exceptions.

Independence.

As mentioned already, if an individual is not self-sufficient, then for such an individual, trying to maintain a stable relationship can become a heavy burden challenging to carry and will probably inhibit an expected success in his relationship with the chosen woman.

Again, if a man has his own goals and financial expectations plus the objective of conquering a woman, he already has half of the success guaranteed.

Something logical in the character of women is that they love a man who depends on himself and whom they can lean on and trust.

It is something like common sense that a woman would feel secure and confident with a man who can provide her physical and emotional security.

Therefore, the ability to transmit security to a woman will not go unnoticed from the beginning of a relationship.

Therefore, a man who makes them feel safe would be someone with a seductive power that does not need words because a woman could feel or perceive that quality in him. Therefore, the independence and reliability of a man are inherent qualities attractive to a woman.

Amiability.

Although it seems somewhat illogical, there is the belief that women are attracted to bad boys. And it is not the generality, but some girls are attracted to unkind men. But this idea often comes from old beliefs that the entertainment media promote.

But one thing is sure desires pass, but gentleness belongs to the personality and is a quality that lasts. And when looking for a serious relationship, women will undoubtedly choose a noble, attentive, and respectful man.

The wonderful thing about kindness is that it is a quality anyone can have or practice.

Another benefit of this quality can be a feeling of mental satisfaction. And such sensations can also help reduce stress levels, which stimulates the body to produce certain hormones such as dopamine, serotonin, etc., strengthening the immunity system and helping relieve anxiety.

Passion.

Finally, a no less critical characteristic is passion, and in a man, passion is an essential element to please a woman.

Without passion, a lover would lack the constant interest on the part of his partner, which would be counterproductive in the pursuit of maintaining the flame of love burning.

Naturally, women deserve love and care, and everything is vital to be considered in the pursuit to make a woman happy. Still, when considering the most needed qualities a man should possess to be a good candidate for a relationship, women expect such a man to have moral ethics as his principles can decisively influence his behavior.

Have you thought about why some people have problems with other people? If you have ever thought about the probable causes.

Then you will also notice that, as a fact, in real life, there are men who do not know how to treat a woman correctly.

However, any man who loves a woman should treat her delicately.

Many women will never say what they want, but by being attentive and sensitive, you can catch the signals she sends. But, of course, you must trust your intuition a little.

In a relationship, communication is vital. Therefore, when a problem arises in the couple, it is best to honestly deal with it so that the relationship can continue the right path.

Do not underestimate the little things. Sometimes they are the ones that matter most to a woman, so pay attention to what she does.

For example, when switching things around, she is trying to attract attention, so let her know that you appreciate her changes. It makes her feel good.

Noticing small details in her clothes or her makeup or hairdo and telling her that she looks beautiful will make her feel good, especially if the compliments are sincere because women need to hear that they are beautiful.

Women deserve attention from the one they love, so no matter if time has passed since the first date, a man should show the same interest from the first day to her.

Not forgetting the special mutual days.

Women do not forget those details and remembering important dates will show her that she continues to be unique to you.

But women also need to know honest opinions about their emotions, ambitions, or fears. So, show that you care about her by listening and being supportive.

Honesty in the couple is the foundation for a solid and lasting relationship. It is also the quality that best speaks of a person's character and values.

Even though being honest sometimes could hurt the feelings of the woman you love, you will never hurt someone more than being dishonest, and a woman deserves to know what it has to do with her.

A woman will always respect an honest man.

By loving your woman, you will love yourself, respect her dignity, and never lie to her.

Respect towards a woman implies that a man will not make her feel inferior because this would be the same as physical or emotional abuse.

No matter the argument, a man must maintain control of himself when discussing the things, he disagrees with the woman in his life.

Giving her the same respect that one expects in the relationship is the proper behavior.

Respect will always be evident in how you treat, communicate with, or refer to her.

A respectful behavior with a woman summarizes more faithfully what it means to be the right man for her.

BEING A FRIEND TO HER

"A friend is one who overlooks your broken fence and admires the flowers in your garden."
— Anonymous

When one feels something for someone, especially towards a woman, one tends to be considerate and kind.

Besides, being kind to the woman you love will invariably make you feel good.

And you can hardly forget someone who had been kind to you.

Whether on the level of friendship or romance. Kindness and respect will always keep us in an optimal relationship with the opposite sex.

A good habit can always be to find the necessary time between occupations to dedicate a short message of affection to the girl that interests you since they always notice those little details.

And maintaining close contact as much as possible will help a woman feel that she is essential in a man's life.

Being affectionate to your partner will always
make a big difference in a relationship. Therefore, be kind to the woman you love.

To have a good friend in life whom you can trust is to be lucky. But if a girl happens to be your best friend, that's almost like a blessing. Making a friendship with a girl has many and varied advantages. Moreover, when it comes to having a good ally in the love aspect, there is no one better than a girl to help you deal with the complexity of conquering a woman's love.

A girl that is your friend will help you with excellent advice and provide you with emotional support.

A male friend can rarely match such loyalty.

Having a sincere friendship with a girl is a blessing for any man. Among other things, a woman can help a man understand the opposite sex more clearly.

If a man has doubts about how a woman thinks or what she is most passionate about, a female friend can make things easier for a man when he tries to approach the chosen woman. The reason is simple, who can better know what a woman thinks is another woman.

Therefore, in matters of romance, a female friend can be the best ally.

Even when a man tries to get the best gift for a girlfriend, the best advice for the perfect gift comes from another girl.

Girls like to help a man when he tries to please a girlfriend. It is something like solidarity.

If you have a girl, bud, it will not be impossible or challenging to conquer your dreams because a female friend will always be willing to help you form a couple with the girl you like.

So, it would be a great idea to make friends with a woman for other special reasons, and if you happen to have already a female friend, be thankful to have that special friendship.

Now how do you become friends with a woman? Making friends with her should not be so complicated if we spontaneously try to start a conversation like with any other person.

Let's consider that what we are looking for is to establish a friendship and that we are not looking for a love relationship which could happen depending on other circumstances.

The first step could be finding common interests and sharing moments.

For example, eating at a restaurant, going to the movies, or accompanying her when she has a problem.

And of course, congratulate her when it is her birthday or a particular day. Even if she moves to live in a faraway place, try to maintain communication on social media as these details will make the friendship with her last in the long run.

Something that unites people a lot is when people can have long conversations to share beliefs and things that they mainly have in common.

The more experiences and intimacies shared, the more bonds of familiarity are formed with a person, especially if this is a woman.

Of course, gaining a woman's trust is extraordinary, so honestly, try to understand her without criticism because the last thing she needs is someone who judges. Communication with understanding is essential for a complete and firm friendship.

Receiving signs of appreciation makes anyone feel good and motivates them to act. However, if you are only friends with her, you should not make her feel uncomfortable with signs of sexual appreciation. Therefore, one must make sure not to be rude or arrogant towards her. Instead, always show her emotional support.

One can tell if a girl is interested in someone romantically by getting acquainted with her. Still, if she is not, it is best to refrain from trying to establish a romantic relationship with her.

The fastest way to end a friendship with a girl is when someone insists on a romantic relationship when she is not interested in the same, which can cause unpleasant tension and discomfort.

However, a friendship between a man and a woman without selfish interests could develop into intimacy, but only if both want it.

All the steps leading to a loving relationship with a woman are essential; therefore, a couple should not underestimate them or take them for granted.

The qualities of friendship between a man and a woman should never change.

Honesty, respect, and care in a friendship relationship are the same qualities a couple will draw on throughout their time together.

When one thinks of a person's qualities we consider a friend, one thinks of how easy it is to talk about anything knowing that there will be no adverse criticism. And one could speak to that person for hours and would not hesitate to come if they needed our presence.

The question is. Shouldn't you give the same attention and importance to the affective relationship with the woman you love and especially when the love relationship has already lasted a long time?

Yet sometimes, couples forget the qualities of friendship that brought them together in the first place.

However, although it requires effort, it is never too late to regain a relationship of affection in courtship or marriage. Still, both parties must be willing to try to repair relationships' damages.

You will have to invest in each other again by paying attention and spending more time together because disconnection cannot rebuild a relationship.

So being in the same place is vital to show that you genuinely care, as both did in the beginning.

So, get excited again, sharing your projects with positive energy as friends do.

The reward of a relationship is greater when apart from love, there is also friendship and support in a profound way where your significant other can feel safer.

LOVE HER MADLY

"Sometimes I wonder if, instead of falling madly in love, we should aspire to fall sanely in love. But then, what would be the point?"
— Jessica Zafra

The study of elements' structure, composition, properties, and energy they produce or absorb when they change is called Chemistry.

This process has often been associated with or compared to the attraction between a man and a woman. And this is something natural in the physical and spiritual sphere.

Therefore, in couple relationships, no one should feel bad when a member of the opposite sex has rejected the other as this is simply because the chemistry was not there as is commonly said.

But when the chemistry is present, that is a very different story because then the signs showing that a strong reaction has taken place are so varied that they leave no room for doubt.

We could mention the body language that is typically very noticeable. For example, such signs are that a man and a woman could find that both have chosen to sit close together or continuously look at each other, among other indications.

And when the steps are complete to establish a love relationship, one must not forget always to show respect so that the relationship can work optimally.

Show her that she is essential in your life.

If there is a misunderstanding, try to clarify things with her gently.

If she wants to cry, the best thing is to hug her telling her that it will be fine and that everything will pass.

If she likes to do something, try to do that activity often.

Consult with her when deciding on something important.

There is a saying that says. Two minds are better than one.

If she makes a mistake in something, forgive, and forget. Because there is no better way to show love to someone, otherwise the relationship will not prosper.

If it is possible to go out together, then go to a place where you both can stay away from the routine, even if it is only for a weekend, the important thing is to spend time together.

Although both have different objectives, support her in her goals. And if something doesn't go as planned, the wise thing to do is to accept your own mistakes by being honest, which will make the relationship more solid.

And whether it is a professional, economic, or family matter, always stay by her side to make her feel strong, knowing that she always can count on you.

If you have already conquered the love of a woman, the opportunities to ingratiate yourself with her are innumerable. Then in those circumstances, making a woman happy depends on you, and it is at this stage that a man's love is verified.

Indeed, no woman resists attention. And there is something that an active woman likes a lot: a foot massage, among other things.

Then, for example, if she has a physical discomfort, get her some medicine to let her know that you care about her well-being.

Also, show her an excellent disposition to help her in anything she may need.

If there is a matter to be discussed, take it seriously, it is not the time to joke.

On the contrary, it is time to listen to her calmly and carefully to solve any situation.

Spending time together is essential for the well-being of the relationship.

Make the moments with that chosen woman pleasant. So, try to look good, exercise, keep fit, shower, shave, put on your best clothes, and do anything that makes you look attractive in her eyes.

Help her as much as possible at home and in her interests, show yourself interested and encouraging.

If something worries or bothers any of you. Talk about it. Please don't waste time ignoring some problem because that detracts from the quality of life together.

If you notice that there are aspects in which you need to improve, work on that, and she will see that you are trying.

Surprise her with flowers, a little message now and then, or give her some small gift. Surprises help keep coexistence in harmony.

And whether both are at home or going to a public place, hold her hand. That will make her feel confident and secure.

Show her that she is the most special person in your life and listen to her when she wants to talk to you about her problems or events in her daily life.

Listen when she expresses her ideas or opinions, always be interested in knowing more about her, and know her points of view.

She likes that you ask her questions, but if you do, do it only to a certain degree without overwhelming her.

Instead, be patient with her.

If you want to take a picture of her, ask her if she would like it to make sure it's okay with her.

In your relationship, call her affectionate names.

And if you give her gifts, do it willingly without expecting her to do the same.

Typically, women are more emotional than men, which does not mean weakness, but it only shows that a woman is precious.

Appreciate her personality. And compliment her beauty. Recognize that she is like a gift from life to you.

In the intimate part of the relationship, do the things you know she likes and tell her that you love her.

Ways in which one can arouse the interest of a woman are diverse, but they all require time and effort.

However, making her fall in love is not everything. The most difficult and important thing is to keep her interested in you.

And so, it is necessary to know the correct ways to treat her, which also implies working on yourself.

By nature, women feel attracted to a self-sufficient and self-confident man.

It is very convenient for a man to work on himself because meeting her needs does not mean giving up doing the things that interest him.

The secret consists of balancing the couple's individual needs so that it can be harmony in the relationship.

Therefore, work on yourself and be optimistic because your optimism will make her feel confident with you.

The quality of your conversations will help her see situations from a different point of view.

Treating a woman as someone equal to yourself is essential instead of trying to exercise control.

Always be courteous and kind to her. Bear in mind that she is a girl and take care of your way of being with her.

In a relationship with a girl, do not take anything for granted. Instead, constantly try to maintain a connection with her by being her friend and respecting her trust.

Allow her to keep her own space so she can always be herself, which means not rushing the relationship.

As stated, be a gentleman and attentive to her since this attitude never goes out of style.

Do not expect unconditional love from her. Instead, allow her to be herself always and support her as much as possible since understanding is what will create the optimal relationship you want.

Loyalty and honesty are two essentials to achieving a genuine and lasting relationship.

And consider that having a woman's love is a responsibility you have now acquired.

However, loving a woman always implies more than one subject.

Therefore, we could also mention that madly loving a woman is not precisely what romance movies portray.

So, the way of loving a woman depends more on each man's character.

Although for many people, love is passion, desire, and need, these feelings are something that diminishes over time.

Eventually, feelings disappear, and couples end their relations to start again with somebody new.

But true love is something different.

Generally, the love that lasts and that can grow more over time is the love that involves commitment.

Among the characteristics of this kind of love is the desire to always stay together. Or do everything possible to stay together.

When the job requires that the man be absent for days, there are two options: go alone or take the spouse with him.

Usually, the man goes alone, but if he travels with his wife, the advantages are many.

Among the advantages of traveling as a couple are that experiences will bring you closer besides, both will be safer taking care of each other.

Individual photos will be more impressive taken by the spouse, even photos taken with the couple posing together.

If someone does not feel well, there will be someone to take care of you.

Responsibilities can be shared, and there will be no better company than the person you love.

One will probably see places one would not see when traveling alone.

Often you get to know more people and places or make more friends when you go somewhere with your partner than when you travel alone.

Sometimes sharing things as a couple when traveling is less expensive.

Of course, there will always be someone with whom to share memories and recall experiences lived together for a long time, among many other things.

Of course, sometimes there are circumstances when traveling as a couple will not be possible but usually traveling with your partner will always be a good idea.

When a woman is a man's priority, the couple will likely always stay and enjoy life together.

So, no matter if a couple is in the beginning stages of friendship or is already married, when lives intertwine deeply as a couple, it is the best sign of true love.

FIGHT FOR HER LOVE DAILY

"We wanted the freedom to love. We wanted the freedom to choose. Now we must fight for it."
— Lauren Oliver, Requiem

Falling in love is the best feeling, and when you find that remarkable woman with whom you want to be always, sometimes it is necessary to fight to keep that love.

A man will do anything for his woman because she is something precious to him.

However, in some cases, you may have to oppose relatives because they don't like the woman you have chosen. But if you love her, your love will remain firm, and you will still decide for her.

Both you and she must be the comfort for each other, letting everyone know that you are genuinely determined to stay together.

Generally, the people around you will accept your relationship with the woman you have chosen, but if this is not the case, fighting for the woman you love is still necessary.

And if you are not hurting someone else, and if it is about just the two of you, then fight for her in every way possible to keep the love of the woman with whom you are happy.

By nature, a woman and a man are different. And both have their ways of showing their love.

It is up to the man to show that he loves his woman by taking the initiative from the beginning. And therein lies the difference.

It happens that sometimes in life, a man finds a woman with whom he lives and although, for some reason, the relationship does not last long, even in memory, said relationship never ends and is always there to make us feel that we have lived.

There are those who keep in memory the best moments of their lives because they have been of simple and total happiness.

If any man has found that remarkable woman, it is time to fight to maintain that relationship.

The truth is that fighting for a relationship implies putting aside pride. However, it is also the time to ask yourself what is required for a relationship to truly last and succeed.

It is also true that when someone has lived with a person for a long time, at some point in the relationship, arguments will arise. Still, you should not be too alarmed because that is perfectly normal in relationships.

Getting angry at one point with your partner is, to a certain extent, healthy for the relationship.

Because a discussion can show that both are interested that the relation works well, it also reinforces the union, and is how you know a little more about the woman you love.

Couple relations are complex because they deal with two different personalities and customs. And sometimes, the family environments have also been different.

Even the most emotionally stable couples go through crises and adjustment problems.

However, it is always worth fighting for the proper functioning of a relationship, which implies accepting each other as they are, accepting the conditions previously established in which both have agreed from the beginning.

So, if problems arise, both should have the maturity to apologize to the other, if necessary, since not doing so, both parties will suffer.

They often could hold resentments by offending each other, although perhaps unintentionally.

To prevent feelings of sadness from forming, it is best to talk and apologize, which is a sign of interest in the well-being of the other.

The apology must be sincere, acknowledging the pain caused. A mutual apology is essential, but you should not require it. To avoid the apology from being misunderstood.

It's best to listen without trying to defend yourself; instead, be patient and respectful.

By being patient, you are showing that you want to resolve the incident because the goal of an apology is to heal the relationship.

Be careful not to mention the incident again to make it clear that you are interested in moving forward with her. Incidents in a couple's relationship require time to heal fully, and it is best to maintain attention and be kind to each other.

Keeping a woman's love is not difficult when you love her. Usually, a woman or girl wants to feel loved, and there are diverse ways in which you can show her that she is loved.

One of those ways is to make her always feel beautiful. It is correct to tell her this because one of the most beautiful things about a woman is that each one is unique.

Sometimes we compare one woman with another, but deep down, we know that no one is like the one you have chosen because each woman has her peculiarities.

Although every woman also knows she is unique, let her know that you appreciate her uniqueness.

Often comfort her by reminding her that she is beautiful.

Hold her hand and be proud of her, respect her clothing choices and the way she wears her hair, and above all, never judge her way of doing her makeup.

If you notice a slight change in her appearance, tell her that you saw something about her and that she looks great.

Tell her that she looks beautiful every chance you get.

Also, recognize her spiritual attributes, looking at her as if you were looking at the most delicate flower.

Remember that for you, she is perfect, and you always want to let her know.

There are days when a woman does not feel so beautiful, and it is the man's job to make her negativity disappear, appreciating and loving her always.

Appreciating the physical and non-physical things about her is what will give the woman you love physical and emotional security.

Although a woman is or looks independent, she will always appreciate a small heroic act from you. Therefore, try to be there when she needs you.

If you and her ever get into a situation, try not to blame her for anything.

Be optimistic and make her laugh because happiness is also a form of love.

Listen to her and be kind to her relatives by being honest with her.

Trust her and don't assume anything.

Get to know her, be optimistic, and learn to love her better by being loyal to her.

Sometimes you will have to make sacrifices. For example, you may sacrifice your ego to love better and keep that woman in your life.

There are times when a man's love for a woman must go through tests, most commonly when the family disapproves of the choice of woman he has made.

Other times a man's love is put to the test when the man must try to understand what makes a woman happy.

Knowing what makes a woman happy is difficult, especially if a man is not the first in a woman's life.

Trying to win a woman's heart is the most challenging task, and more complex than achieving the acceptance of the man's family is performing the conquest and maintenance of a woman's love in the long term.

And is that managing to maintain the love of a woman, if not easy, is not impossible either, but character and some other factors are required to maintain the love of a woman you do not want to lose.

The truth is a woman's love is never totally conquered but keeping a woman's love requires continuously showing her that her man loves her.

Therefore, what is needed are only small but powerful things done with honesty.

Among the little things, that day by day can conquer a woman's heart is the genuine interest in her day. Listening to whatever she has to say, going out to dinner, and letting her know she looks beautiful are among the things every woman needs.

Of course, in addition to physical needs, a woman needs emotions and feelings like listening and knowing that you love her for everything she is.

In a gentle voice, she needs to hear that life is better because of her.

Little affectionate touches and looking into her eyes will tell her best what she needs to know.

In general, she needs to know that you appreciate who she is intellectually, emotionally, and physically.

Do not forget that a fact says more than a thousand words and showing a woman that she is worth a lot is another form of good intimacy in a constant struggle to maintain the love of the woman you love.

A GENTLEMAN ALWAYS

"A gentleman knows when to call her sexy, and when to let her know she's beautiful."

—Anonymous

Some things never go out of style, and being a gentleman is one of them, but this attitude implies more than beliefs, actions, or dressing.

The actual values of a gentleman are what set a man apart. For a gentleman, chivalry is a way of being unlike other men.

So even his clothing will reveal his character, and his relaxed attitude will draw people's attention, especially women.

No matter the circumstances, a gentleman will always act accordingly to his character.

Surprisingly, even a modern woman still will recognize a man's chivalry. The reason is that chivalry is never out of fashion and practicing chivalry doesn't take much.

Chivalry is not dead. And simple acts of kindness and care done for a man, such as opening a door, pulling out a chair, or offering his coat to a girl on a chilly evening, is a sign of the high esteem a man holds for his lady.

Moreover, a gentleman always finds happiness in being of service to a woman.

Also, a gentleman doesn't expect something in return but gets pleasure in helping others.

In the modern world today. Where trouble and confusion can distort the concept of being a gentleman, the right thing to do is reexamine what it takes to be a gentleman.

Though it is nothing new, it may still be hard to accept some of the most important concepts about being a gentleman, such as the fact that a man should never tell or speak ill about other people. Instead, he will protect his integrity as well as the integrity of the ones around himself.

So, discretion is vital.

Working for your achievements will provide greater satisfaction later. A gentleman knows that he owns that for which he has worked only.

A gentleman doesn't have to be a dance expert, but he knows the basic steps to ensure he can enjoy a moment with his woman.

When a person needs a little help the gentlemanly thing to do is offer some slight assistance.

When someone invites a gentleman to a party, he brings something to share with other guests.

A gentleman chooses confidence instead of arrogance.

The concept of chivalry is still alive today.

In essence, chivalry is about good manners, empathy, forgiveness, and always speaking the truth.

A policy that always works is honesty. And though it may seem insensitive a gentleman will always go to the point while avoiding judging anyone.

Of course, no matter the company, a gentleman is always well-presented. When making a handshake, he will immediately make eye contact that tells the people about his character.

Being a gentleman always and everywhere with other people is an excellent and correct behavior any man should strive to practice. However, it is with the woman near whom a man should strive to display chivalry.

So, whether a woman is your wife or girlfriend, show her that you appreciate her opinions.

Again, making eye contact with her when she is trying to explain something will show that you genuinely pay attention.

Be polite and avoid cursing or other ugly expressions when talking with her because good manners can ensure a long and pleasurable relationship.

Making a genuine question or giving a fine compliment is a great and simple way to start a conversation with a woman. And when she talks, let her finish her speech, avoiding interrupting her, no matter if you have something important to say. This way, you will be proving that you appreciate her thoughts.

If she sends you a message don't make her wait too long and complete your return reply politely and precisely.

Also, when you have a date with her try to be on time or even early if you can.

Though dressing sharp makes a notable difference not always is possible to have designer clothing. Then a simple good shower, combed hair, and a clean outfit can be enough for a good impression.

Because it is unpolite with your date, try to keep your phone silent when you are with her.

When you take her home walk with her to her door, ensuring she gets safely in the house.

Finally, when you walk with her down the street. Allow her to walk next to the wall. So, you will be acting as a shield protecting her from a drunk motorist or some other danger.

Protecting her on the street is undeniable proof that you value her safety, which is the most remarkable example of chivalry.

Chivalry is an excellent attitude, and it is equally important to consider other aspects in the attempt to start a successful relationship with a woman.

An old advice that never goes out of style when treating a woman is to be a gentleman.

Indeed, being a gentleman involves more than buying her flowers, pulling up a chair for her, opening the door, or giving her your jacket on a cold afternoon.

Chivalry is good and perfectly normal, and nothing is wrong with it.

However, even if a man behaves this way, it does not guarantee that a woman will accept him.

The reason is that what primarily attracts a woman to a man is sexual attraction, and when this element is missing, what a woman will feel will be a pleasant, friendly emotion but nothing more.

Therefore, if a man does not exert a type of sexual attraction on a woman, it will not matter how chivalrous such a man is with her.

Only when a man has ignited the sexual spark in a woman will she truly begin to appreciate the chivalry and good intentions of such a man towards her.

Although gentlemanly behavior is worthy of praise, it is not what attracts a woman to a man.

This revelation is unfortunate because good manners are excellent when trying to impress a woman, but the reality and results are different.

However, movies and television have promoted that chivalry is excellent for attracting women, but things don't work that way in real life.

Chivalry is indeed a behavior innately appreciated by women. Still, if a gentleman cannot arouse sexual attraction in a woman, his chivalry will only be chivalry, but not romantic interest.

The truth is that in most successful relationships. Even at the beginning of the relationship, there is already a sexual attraction. So, it does not take much time to get to the sex.

In the past, most women had to get married before having sexual intercourse. Therefore, they spent a lot of time treating a man, and the choice of the best candidate to be a husband depended mainly on the chivalry displayed by the candidate.

However, now women no longer depend so much on a man because now the woman is more and more independent, and now they can decide with whom to have a relationship.

Now even if a woman is not satisfied with a partner, she can end it and start another relationship with someone else.

Likewise, men don't need much chivalry and time to conquer a woman sexually, but even if a man insists on being polite with a woman, that's just something extra.

Also, for the modern man, the concept of chivalry is more like an attitude that denotes class when interacting with women.

Meanwhile, although a man's chivalry can impress a woman, this attitude will not take the man very far if there is no sexual attraction involved.

Without sexual attraction, a man's chivalry will be something irritating to her, which will also make her feel angry.

So, she will go without hesitation to be interested in another man.

There is nothing wrong with a gentlemanly attitude. Still, if a man seeks to conquer a woman's love, he must openly express his intentions for her and not act as if he was only interested in friendship.

Not being afraid to express a man's interest in a woman is one of the best attitudes to be successful at the beginning of a relationship.

On the other hand, some women are also insecure about themselves and need to know clearly when a man is interested in them.

So good manners are excellent; however, if a man cannot exert sexual attraction to a woman, he will not be more than a friend.

But the sexual attraction will have to be honest because if it is not as a relationship progresses, a woman will realize that a man is only trying to impress her with his good manners.

She will then make it impossible for such a man to advance beyond being just another friend.

Most men naturally have something of a gentleman in themselves already.

So, when trying to start a relationship with a woman, a man should begin by creating a sexual attraction first.

If he manages to exercise said attraction on her, everything else, including chivalry, will flow spontaneously.

BECAUSE YOU CAME IN PEACE, LEAVE IN PEACE

"It is not enough to win a war; it is more important to organize the peace."

— Aristotle

The bottom line of any relationship is friendship, and goodwill on both sides or parties involved.

And it is in the love relationship between a man and a woman where politeness, courtesy, and friendship are essential to start such relationship.

But when in the couple, one of the two decides to end the relationship. How could this decision be communicated without causing much pain?

It is never easy to say goodbye to someone you have loved. However, when the end is inevitable, all that remains is facing the situation and continuing with life itself.

Although ending a relationship can be overwhelming, you can do certain things to make the breakup respectful and honest.

It is best not to spend too much time trying to avoid the situation because delaying the already decided rupture will only hurt both parties more.

Trying to make the conversation healthy, explain the reason for the breakup without being very specific, use kindness and avoid lying, remembering that what is needed is also to maintain future mental health.

Consequently, there will likely be negative mental states and sadness after the breakup, but it is best to try to maintain your life as usual as possible, avoiding more stress than you should.

Little by little, try to rebuild your life by focusing on yourself, trying new things, spending time with family and friends, and eventually, you will be ready for love again.

However, if breaking up is inevitable, the fairest and most honorable thing is to try to end a relationship in the best possible terms of goodwill and peace.

Unfortunately, not always a relationship ends in a friendly manner, although it should.

When a man and a woman start a relationship is generally always with the best intentions and on good terms. And both put their best effort into making an honest, polite, and kind start.

Therefore, the end of a relationship should not have a bitter taste but rather be a process in cordial terms of friendship without trying to offend each other and much less allow hatred.

When we fall in love, we expect it to be the best decision in life, and we hope it lasts.

Unfortunately, for various reasons, sometimes something happens, and the relationship ends.

The most common reasons why a relationship ends can be that those involved realize that their personalities are not related, lack of time to be together, infidelity, and sexual dissatisfaction, can be some of the causes.

And so, it becomes necessary to know how to make this breakup transition as least damaging as possible for both parties.

Ending a relationship with someone you loved is not an easy thing.

First, you need to understand that the end of a relationship will always be painful for both parties but knowing this will help you prepare for the moods and feelings to come.

Although it will be equally painful, it is advisable to communicate the decision to break up in person out of consideration for the person with whom we have shared part of our life.

And unless you fear backlash from the other party, a public place such as a cafe or park would be the safest choice for this conversation.

When we talk about a breakup, it is best to speak honestly without offering many details. Saying a lot of it risks hurting the self-esteem or dignity of the person who has been our partner.

When explaining the reasons for the breakup, it is best to take care of each of our words without using trite expressions. But just simply and clearly express our decision.

Now, this is not the time to start arguments because when you have reached this point in the relationship, it is for a reason, and trying to offer too many explanations will only make the farewell more difficult.

When the couple has reached this moment of parting, it is best to try to be kind and considerate, focusing the conversation on the other person so that things are easier for both.

For now, it is best to avoid emotions by mentioning the good or bad things from the past because it is not about restoring or looking for someone to blame. Instead, express the decision courteously.

The truth is that regardless of who decides to end the relationship, both parties will go through a period of longing, sadness, and pain.

However, it would help if you remembered why the relationship did not work to adapt to the new circumstances.

Staying busy with study, work, and family will help overcome the breakup.

Maintaining a positive attitude is essential, but if the sadness persists, know it is entirely normal.

The following comment is not intended as advice but is only a commentary on something real.

A love break does not have to end goodwill that started as a friendship in a moment when someone was looking for something that perhaps they didn't have.

From a time. When there were only two, and one depended on the other.

When being with a loved one, good and bad memories happen in our life, then we can say that we have lived just because someone chose us among so many other people.

Only two things can happen at the end of a relationship between a man and a woman.

It could be that they never see each other again in their lives, or, despite the separation, they continue in contact through messages and sporadic chats over the years.

And sometimes, no matter the passing of time, they can still be able to talk about the good times and the things they lived together.

But this is possible only when the two are willing to maintain the memories alive in their lives.

This time without looking for or expecting anything else but from the other but just knowing that one has a friend to talk to sometimes.

A, although this may not lead precisely to a place anywhere.

Nevertheless, it is still better to have such a friendship than to have died in the memory of a person who was once dear.

This type of relationship is very unusual, although it can exist because some people are uniquely different than most people.

There is a phrase that honestly reflects the truth that we all should follow when starting or ending a deal between a man and woman and is the following.

(When you enter or leave someone's life, close the door affectionately).

Unfortunately, being kind and honest is something that we, the people, difficultly or rarely practice in our lives because of a lack of character and honesty.

When a relationship doesn't work out, and those involved find it necessary to end it, sometimes this fact is downplayed.

People forget that relationships always begin with warmth, affection, hope, and enthusiasm.

So, the end of a relationship should also include compassion, respect, and even a little love.

And whether you want to keep the friendship or not, undoubtedly, there will still be friends, family, and other people who have known you.

For this reason, a couple should break the relationship with kindness because this is the best way to proceed to continue life without bad resentments.

The end of a relationship where respect and honesty are present will allow the couple to maintain inner peace and emotional stability after the break-up, making the separation process less painful.

It takes effort and dedication to start a relationship, and it also takes effort and commitment to end it, no matter the relationship's level.

It also requires honesty and courage to clearly express to the couple the decision and steps to take after the breakup.

However, consideration focused on respect and understanding is the best way to close this chapter of life.

WHEN THE BEST IS GOING ALONE

"I used to think the worst thing in life was to end up all alone, it's not. The worst thing in life is to end up with people that make you feel all alone."

– Unknown

When you have tried to stay in a relationship, and still, you keep finding reasons that make that relationship impossible, it is time to seriously consider why it is not working and, consequently, realize that the best is to walk out of it.

No matter how much you loved that person.

The perfect partner should be someone with whom you have affinities, who you can trust, who has similar goals, and who you are willing to try everything.

It is not very difficult to realize if someone is the ideal person you expect.

Sometimes you can feel it, and if you can't handle it,

but on the contrary, you feel sad when you should feel excited and happy.

So, the best thing is not to continue with someone you thought you loved.

Perhaps there are doubts regarding intuition but answering a few questions could help you see more clearly if it is convenient to continue with that relationship.

Are there constant discussions about the same topics? Is it difficult for you to be yourself with your partner? Are the expectations between you and your partner different? or is there no interest of one of the parties in committing? If your answers indicate that your goals are going in another direction other than your partner's, then you might be better off starting on your own.

Sometimes fear prevents us from starting to live on our own, but if we continue in an unfulfilling relationship, that fear will only lead to a life of unhappiness.

Often during courtship, we see minor signs that tell us that something is not logical or is what we expect.

And with the hope that things will change with time, we refuse to accept that something is not correct.

Until one day, we experience damage and hurt, which almost always begins with a lack of respect toward us.

That's why it's essential to realize when it's time to let go of the things that hurt us.

And thus, avoid further damage.

To keep moving forward with our lives and still be able to maintain mental health.

Life is about maintaining a balance between what we want and what is good for us, but making the right decisions is not always easy, especially when we try to love somebody who we are not sure is the best for us.

An optimal relationship between a man and a woman allows them to develop as a couple and helps them grow individually.

But if in the relationship there are no strong ties that unite them and help develop a good life as a couple, perhaps you are living with the wrong person.

Although if this is the case, it does not have to be the end of everything.

When ending a relationship is the emotional healing, the one that takes the longest to repair.

Sometimes having lived a long or short relationship doesn't change the amount of emotional damage.

Usually, the hurting is always the same and makes it difficult to recover.

In some cases, healing takes more time than others.

People have a natural tendency to relate to other people, and this disposition not only has emotional advantages since healthy relationships are proven to help to faster recovery from illnesses and strengthens the immune system.

Consequently, most men and women seek cordial and lasting relationships, and when this objective is not successfully reached, negative feelings and states arise.

Nevertheless, people can still have a reasonably good life without depending emotionally on someone.

Happiness is something one creates and depends on how one perceives life regardless of the circumstances.

Therefore, even after the end of a love relationship, you can still be happy, although the process of returning to the state before the connection is not so easy.

But some things can help you survive the breakup.

And being able to return to an excellent state of mind and positivity is well worth it.

The first step to healing emotional wounds is not to shy away from the pain you feel but rather accept it as part of a circumstance that will eventually pass since an experience of this type is also part of life.

Feeling the pain from the separation shows that you have been happy, and unconsciously you want to return to those happy states but facing these vivid feelings will help you overcome the sadness.

Now the goal is to get out of this state of pain and not let this feeling continue indefinitely, and for this reason, you must try to keep yourself busy with things that give you optimism. Perhaps now you can start something you haven't tried until now.

You could, for example, write a story or a poem, start studying a new language, make a little trip, or talk to a friend with whom you feel confident.

Whatever you decide to do, do it with sincerity, which will help you let go of what is now weighing on your mind.

Try to see your situation from an external point of view and see what conclusions you reach.

One thing that will help you get your spirits back, in the long run is to try not to harbor resentment so that you will eventually be able to start over.

Above all, forgive what you must forgive yourself and move on with your life and remember that being happy depends primarily on you only.

Positive emotions are good for our mind and body, reducing stress and anxiety, which is well-being.

And from a general point of view, everyone occasionally goes through a period of sadness.

Still, no matter what has caused us pain, there will always be reasons to feel happy, and the best way to maintain happiness is to have a good attitude when times are difficult.

Because just like everyone else, you deserve a healthy and happy life too.

Even when you are already in a relationship, there are times when it is necessary to analyze yourself with specific questions, such as how you feel being in your relationship.

Do you feel free, happy, calm, or excited?

But if, on the contrary, you feel alone even though technically you are not, but if the feeling of loneliness persists, perhaps you should analyze the causes in more detail.

If you feel better without your partner, maybe you're in the wrong relationship. However, not having a partner shouldn't be the worst situation of your life.

According to research, there are also physical and mental benefits for those who decide to remain single.

To begin with, being alone, you learn to depend on yourself, and by doing so, you will no longer need to rush into starting another relationship with a likely wrong person.

Sometimes, the fear of loneliness makes us rush to seek someone's company.

However, if you take your time staying alone, you will discover that time is a great healer that will help you leave the past behind.

Even alone, you can take advantage of your time to get to know new places, and it also allows you to learn a lot about yourself.

Studies show that single people exercise more than married people to be physically fit and healthy.

Among other things, if your circumstances are being single, that prevents you from more chances to get in a bad mood or feeling guilty about a discussion with your partner.

Staying single, you can concentrate on your work or study, knowing that no one is affected by your occupations. You could also start a relationship spontaneously if the opportunity arises and decide without pressure if he-she is the person you want in your life.

Something very sure is that people will need to be self-sufficient at some stage.

However, if they have never experienced this circumstance, loneliness could produce feelings of resentment when they must go through this reality.

So, when a relationship is not correct for one of the parties involved, it is best to continue by yourself.

Being on your own does not mean the end of the world because each unfortunate circumstance can also bring positive qualities if, in some way, we are aware or prepared to go through such a personal stage.

THERE IS A REASON THEY ARE CALLED AFFAIRS

"You didn't just cheat on me; you cheated on us. You didn't just break my heart; you broke our future."

— Steve Marabolik

An affair or infidelity is a sexual relationship outside the marital arrangement.

The reality is that the betrayal of one of the partners does not lead to something positive, and it does show the world that there has been a severe problem with oneself.

It also shows a profound deficiency of a person's character; whatever is said is never an accident and there is almost always damage to third parties.

Strange as it may seem, some will not hide their intentions to betray, although the price to pay for an adventure will always be too high.

Although reasons should not be valid, whoever betrays their spouse do so for specific reasons, though after the affair, nothing can ever be the same again.

And both men and women commit infidelity for one reason or another.

It may be that the couple does not spend enough time together, and one of the two abuse the spouse, forcing one of them to seek affection elsewhere.

Therefore, in this case, anyone would become unfaithful by having the opportunity to seek someone else to make the man or woman feel desired or wanted.

However, infidelity also occurs in couples who could be said to enjoy a solid union and are happy.

The truth is that infidelity is inherent in men and women. Although one of the spouses can be faithful, perhaps the other spouse in the couple cannot.

Some say that infidelity does not necessarily require one of the couples to have extramarital relations.

Because from the moment one of the two flirts with another man or woman who is not the spouse.

From that moment, a person is already an unfaithful person.

And the fact is that sooner or later, one of the two fails to be faithful.

Perhaps the unfaithful will find excuses to minimize this attitude or behavior, which will try to make one feel less guilty. Still, in the end, it will only be a way to excuse a tendency in their personality.

The reasons why both sexes come to commit infidelity may differ, but what does not change is that both sexes get to commit adultery.

Sometimes we talk about the causes and the percentage of couples who fail in their relationships. Yet, surveys found that up to twenty percent of men and thirteen percent of women admit to being unfaithful to their spouses.

Other research shows that in most couples where one of the two has been unfaithful, divorce immediately, and other partners remain together but eventually end in separation.

And those that do not eventually end up separating.

And only a few couples survive infidelity by staying together.

The foundation of a love affair is a strong but temporary feeling towards the desired person, a feeling which is contrary to sincere love.

The truth is that those involved in an affair spend very little time together, and usually, it is not the best decision for no one.

And the adventure itself is a draining emotional load instead of being a state of tranquility and comfort.

It is enough to mention only some of the consequences of infidelity to recognize that being unfaithful to your spouse is wrong.

By committing infidelity, one risks losing the person who has been a fundamental part of one's life.

And among other things, one risks peace of mind, economic position, the well-being of children, and the loyalty of the only person who otherwise would continue to give its support, even in the worst of times.

Marriage is the decision to live a monogamous life with a spouse, and committing infidelity is the betrayal of that relationship.

And then it doesn't matter how much you think you love the other person.

At first, the lie will require secrecy to cover up more lies which will make the emotion of the moment unpleasant, and in the long run, embarrassment and worry will create a feeling of unhappiness that will remain for an endless time.

And comparing the life one had before the betrayal will make you miss the love, values, and esteem you previously enjoyed.

And realizing that the adventure wasn't worth it will make the infidel feel only more miserable.

A topic often forgotten by those who decide to get involved in an affair of infidelity is sexual and even mental health.

In addition, the greater the number of intimate partners, the greater the risk of contracting a venereal disease.

To be discovered and confronted with the lie before the spouse is an unpleasant experience full of shame and humiliation.

And from then on, nothing will be the same because, in addition to a probable divorce, resentment will create a terrible situation that will remain so indefinitely.

Also, the damage to the betrayed spouse's self-esteem will prevent them from trusting someone else again, and the doubt will accompany them for the rest of their life.

Most people behold the infidel with disdain, and although the family does not say so deep down, everyone will criticize that mistake, not to mention there will be those who will, in secrecy, make fun of it.

However, the criticism of the people around will be the least severe problem because a betrayal of one of the spouses will be a humiliation and create confusion, insecurity, and sadness in their children. The cheater will lose all moral authority.

As if all this were not enough, in the future, an explanation will have to be given to a future husband or wife when they want to start another relationship.

If the answer is not honest, perhaps new lies will be resorted to, which will create a labyrinth of doubts in the mind of the new prospect causing conflicts that will make the new relationship difficult.

And in this way, the consequences of infidelity will continue to affect life over time.

There will be couples who survive infidelity but not without suffering or harming first to someone innocent.

There will also be those who will say that it is best to analyze the relationship and determine if you want to fix what is wrong or end the relationship that will eventually end anyway.

But whether you will continue with the relationship, it is best to discuss this with your partner first and agree on what you want to do about it before deciding to start something new with someone else.

Supposing a couple decides to end their relationship or marriage.

In that case, both can continue their lives separately, and no one can blame or make anyone feel guilty because of adultery and its unfavorable consequences.

Generally, an affair is a relationship based on sex that, in turn, is usually of short duration.

Some investigations affirm that said relationship can last between a few months or even two years, although rare exceptions exist.

An affair and a marriage relationship are very different.

A relationship with commitment and honesty can last a lifetime due to the moral or spiritual connection between two people.

Also, an affair always has consequences that affect the ones practicing it and those around them.

Infidelity affects not only the couple but also the children, not to mention the psychological pain, mental health, chronic stress, and the inevitable depression in all those affected.

Unfortunately, the effects can be long and devastating.

Although not mentioned frequently or enough, infidelity does not have happy endings.

Extramarital affairs have in common that they are shrouded in conflicting emotions and feelings such as misery, danger, unhappiness, excitement, and drama.

But soon, what is new ceases to be, excitement little by little ages and dies, and the new flesh ceases to be unique, and when you already have what you thought new, the attraction becomes a routine like the one from which you wanted to escape before.

The truth is that those involved in infidelity do not know each other because the emotion they felt at the possibility of cheating on their spouse blinded them. Still, now they can see more clearly and see that the attraction has turned into frustration.

At the beginning of a relationship, when people only talk about the positive aspects, they think they have, they can never get to know the other completely.

In a daily environment, couples can appreciate how they are with all their flaws that during the date stage weren't fully exposed.

When the true personality suddenly appears. There can be explosions of characters that seem to have come out of nowhere.

Although the flaws had always been there and until now, they reveal.

When the passion and excitement naturally begin to wane, the need to pay attention again to other more vital aspects of life begins to grow. Enchantment begins to fade, primarily when the initial attraction lies in chemical appeal.

Then states of grief, remorse, and depression become prevalent in daily life.

The remaining option for one or both members of the affair is to leave each other only to start again with somebody new.

If we put aside the moral aspects, we could conclude that a love affair can leave a helpful lesson on what to choose as individuals when we already have a life with a partner.

One could see oneself more clearly and then act with more wisdom and decision.

Whatever the decision that one makes concerning the spouse, it is good to know the consequence of our actions. In the case of an affair, it will be possible to weigh whether infidelity is worth it, or it is better to decide to be a better person for everyone around us by staying loyal and honest.

MARRIED LIFE

"A perfect marriage is just two imperfect people who refuse to give up on each other."

– Unknown

Wanting to commit your life to another person is the basis of marriage. However, marital success will depend on the decisions made daily.

Commitment is the choice of future goals with the spouse aimed at a common benefit.

Marriage will be much more than dates, conversations, meals, fun, or endless affection.

More than anything, marriage means work and commitment.

Quality time with the spouse will show a commitment to them.

It will be necessary to remind oneself of the positive aspects of the spouse constantly. Also, a strong relationship will require having a positive and consistent spirit to make the relationship flourish.

Marriage is like an adventure composed of happy and sometimes sad moments with the person you love in which both are responsible for each other.

In return, this responsibility provides them with a good and satisfying life.

In addition, the union between man and woman becomes the basis of the society in which they live.

When marriage's value is subject to debate, the consequences of divorce and the resulting harm are invariably also discussed.

Research shows that children whose parents face divorce are more likely to fall into poverty, experience abuse from strangers, drop out of school, use drugs, or engage in premature sexual activity, and deteriorate physically and mentally.

As a result, they can become adults with serious problems.

On the contrary, a strong marriage can protect children.

It can also prepare them to be happy adults and integrate them into a productive and functional society.

Something not mentioned very often is that a lot of literature teaches what the Bible has always affirmed.

"It is not good for a man to be alone," And therefore, neither is for the woman.

Research reveals that people within the marriage bond live longer and lead fuller and more satisfying lives than those divorced or in a free union.

One benefit of living within the marriage is the lower risk of suffering violence, including domestic violence, since boyfriends instead of husbands commit higher rates of violence.

Also, according to statistics, married couples live longer and enjoy better physical health. And even the children of married couples live longer and enjoy better health.

Marriage is a tremendous legal institution; for those involved, it can also symbolize commitment, privilege, and personal fulfillment.

Ultimately, marriage strengthens the bond between parents and children.

In addition, marriage is generally the institution that consistently receives the support of the family and the community.

Marriage is the learning place of moral values that will eventually give life purpose and meaning to life.

It is in a marriage where both parties that form it pursue the same objective of protecting other lives, guiding themselves to live more.

Marriage is also a transforming act because it creates a commitment to sexual fidelity by a couple, an economic union, and a parental alliance.

Marriage is an alliance formed due to the desire expressed before an institution to change two individual lives for a life of commitment as a couple.

A successful marriage is not by chance. Instead, its base is love and respect, although each party involved must do their part daily.

Commitment in a marriage involves much more than the desire to stay together through life's ups and downs.

Instead, it is a steadfast desire to remove doubts that the marriage relationship is a temporary experiment.

The part love has in marriage must be generously reinforced with sacrifice to sustain that feeling, giving of oneself without expectation of reward and forgiving each other for mistakes.

And the best way to avoid mistakes is to communicate clearly and often.

Talking with your spouse about any subject is the best way to maintain a healthy relationship, and respectfully listening to your spouse's opinion and ideas, and taking time to understand their needs, is part of good communication.

Being grateful daily and appreciating each other will help the relationship significantly.

Keep the romance factor alive by planning dates as much as possible and enjoying each other's company.

Just as spending time as a couple is important, spending time alone is also necessary.

Spouses tend to forget personal interests, but going out with friends occasionally, taking classes, or practicing a hobby help enrich lives and help to appreciate the presence of the spouse more.

Naturally, every couple may have disagreements. But even in these cases, it is essential to be impartial and respectful.

Try listening to the spouse's point of view, avoiding anger or frustration, trying to calm down, and finding another time to discuss the problems from another perspective. Giving both a little is the best way to solve problems.

Researchers find that there are some serious threats to marriage, and among them are thoughtlessness, distrust, and lack of dialogue.

Staying away from these harmful tendencies will allow the marriage to become and remain solid.

Couples who refrain from hostilities and resort to gentleness and responsibility for their actions are the ones who best repair problems in their relationship.

Everyone makes mistakes, so knowing how to forgive and forget the offense is necessary without constantly bringing it to mind, especially with your partner.

Even the happiest couples have discussions because no marriage can always be satisfied.

There are always ups and downs.

However, there are also ways to overcome crises.

If a couple is going through difficult times, it does not necessarily mean they are unhappy. It is something normal.

You must be well and continue forward because no one is exempt from misunderstandings.

Maintaining the commitment to the spouse and the family is essential to building a life as a couple.

Marriage relationships can grow significantly over time, but strengthening the foundations always is the basis for a lasting marriage.

Sometimes the routine in the life of a couple can become stressful.

However, simple things like laughing together even in the face of problems can help both see life with optimism, and when both can show a sense of humor, their marital ties grow.

Creating good moments in the couple is not so difficult, and it is already an advantage to live together because the spouses can express their appreciation to each other every day.

Showing constant appreciation for one's spouse can ward off any possible resentment or estrangement in the marriage.

Growing together in marriage requires both of you to be willing to adapt to changes brought about by needs and circumstances to mature individually and as a couple until death does you part.

Married life is like a long journey where two people keep each other company along the way that will be full of challenges and hard work, but on this travel, there will also be pleasant and happy moments.

Just like when traveling to some distant country, it will take faith that you can get to your destination and a determination not to give up and encourage each other that success is possible.

A happy married life is only possible if the couple has understanding, mutual dignity, and tolerance.

Like the Biblical saying that asks the question. Would two walk the same path if both disagree? And the answer is that they must agree to walk together to arrive happily at their destination.

In marriage, both spouses are different. However, these differences can also be favorable because both can take advantage of each other's individual qualities.

The harmony of a good marriage allows the couple to turn their home into a pleasant place and the enthusiasm in both helps them forgive each other their faults and overcome problems better.

The honest interaction of the couple can help to enjoy a healthy relationship, and the marriage can grow through sharing emotions.

A committed marriage should make the couple happy because both will realize that their differences are also elements that are part of marriage, and if the couple shares the same objectives, they can reach their goals.

Of course, healthy married life requires a safe and stable environment.

Often, couples at the beginning of life together lack certain comforts or needs, but this is where love and understanding work in the couple's favor to provide for all these necessities for a fuller life.

Therefore, married life cannot always be full of happiness, but with commitment, honesty, and understanding, a couple can achieve the goals for a happy married life.

TRUE STATUS OF A MAN

"Real men don't conform to the beliefs of others, even when society has concluded on what is good and true but maintain the integrity of their own mind."
– Ralph Waldo Emerson

Science still discusses the different factors that make a woman feel attracted to a man, and science still does not reach a general agreement.

There may not be a general reason, but different factors make a woman feel attracted to a particular man.

Although this attraction also depends on a particular woman.

Among the causes that can influence interest in a man by a woman are, among others, the excellent appearance of a well-dressed man.

But there are several, and some of these factors are sometimes beyond our control since not all men have the same physical and genetic conditions such as testosterone levels, social perceptions, etc.

Fortunately, other factors could be within reach of any man that as well attract women.

Those factors include lifestyle, occupation, physical appearance, self-sufficiency, and behavior.

The factors are many and diverse. However, often, a critical factor perceived as an essential quality by many women is if a man belongs to a higher social status.

Therefore, it is not surprising to note that social position is most considered when considering a partner.

When talking about status, the economic resources of a person, expensive clothing, and dominant behavior are usually considered, among others.

However, it seems that the chances of a man's success are what makes him considered attractive by women, the same as the already influential position of another man.

A man's social status can determine his sexual attraction to women.

But above all, what determines a man's attraction is how he perceives himself, especially with women.

Therefore, the desire to attract women will determine a man's behavior, and he will try all the possibilities to obtain the acceptance of certain types of women.

On the other hand, other men will just be themselves without expecting to appear too attractive to women. Still, since their behavior will be more natural, some women will see them as appealing.

By nature, a man who trusts in himself behaves in a certain way that simultaneously makes him perceived as attractive because the physique, clothes, and style are simply the result of what he is inside.

Therefore, the essential traits of an attractive man are his self-confidence.

Although he does not dismiss the impression that the people around him have of him.

Something to mention about a confident man's traits is his ability to stay positive at most times.

As an example of a confident man's optimistic personality, we could mention that jealousy is not one of his characteristics because he is clear about the kind of woman who interests him.

And honestly, he can express his sexual desire to the woman he loves.

He knows that he is not perfect and feels confident.

Treating the woman with respect, he enjoys with her and is happy without seeking to impress anyone.

The positive behavior of this kind of man is what primarily makes him attractive in the eyes of most women.

However, it is necessary to mention the behavior of certain men who, due to insecurities, experience more problems than happiness.

Some examples of insecurity include calling a woman excessively, trying desperately to impress her, not accepting rejection, lying too much when dealing with the opposite sex, and exercising control in the relationship.

The truth is that when intentions are honest and your interest in a woman is genuine, you are more likely to attract equally open women.

In other words, attraction depends not on looking attractive but on being genuine.

Other elements of attraction that are worth mentioning and often used by men to attract women sexually are chivalry, gentleness, acts of bravery, and even the demonstration of desire directed explicitly towards her.

Generally, men of action who display bravery daily in their lives exert a sexual attraction on women more effectively than men with stock trades.

Often men of action tend to be gallant and, at the same time, rough who do not hide what they want and resolutely pursue their goals.

On the contrary, regular men tend to show insecurity by not approaching women, asking them out, or being afraid to accompany them, which is something that more surely will disappoint them.

But if the way to approach a woman is respectful, there would be no need to worry about her reaction because it is more likely that she will respond positively to your interest in her.

Some examples based on experience that work to approach a girl include, for example, telling a woman that she is pretty and then waiting for her reaction, which will generally be pleasant and will result in a free path to get to know her better.

When it happens that a woman is interested in you, simply holding her hand will be enough to start a romantic relationship.

When a woman agrees to go out with you, it is possible to determine what type of relationship you can aspire to with her soon.

Men often underestimate the qualities they naturally possess to approach and attract women already attracted to them.

Fundamentally it is important to know why one should behave in a certain way instead of another.

Because in communication with a woman, the motives are as important as the behavior itself.

Therefore, achieving a good impression of a woman to attract her depends on the degree of security shown before her, and her favorable reaction will only result from the behavior displayed.

However, it is necessary to accept that despite trying everything, a man still can be subject to rejection by women but recognizing this truth will help to avoid feeling disappointed.

The true success derived from interacting with women is to honestly be able to enjoy the relationship with one of them.

And true enjoyment comes from an internal emotional process rather than external factors.

Obtaining the status of genuine attraction depends on investing and taking care of oneself.

This internal emotional process will result in the quality of the beautiful woman that can come into a man's life.

There are attributes that women look for in a man.

Although every man has individual characteristics, some qualities set them apart as a class making them attractive to women.

However, though times change, some things never change, and one of those things is that a woman needs to be loved by a man.

So, in the end, what a woman wants and needs from the man she loves is to feel loved and protected by him, and we could say that this need will never change.

Also, a man in the full extension of the word will always accept his role of lover and protector of her, equally displaying tenderness, vitality, and character, which are the qualities that will make him attractive in the eyes of any woman.

However, a woman usually can perceive if a man loves her, and she will not hesitate to control her affections and even end a relationship if a man's love is not genuine.

On the other hand, when a woman believes someone is the ideal man for her, she will fight for her relationship.

Of course, such a man must be interested in her with honesty.

There are examples of authentic men who are lovers and family men who also have a wife who greatly helps the relationship's success.

Although some women try to take advantage of the men they meet, they are not the majority.

The belief that women only want handsome and financially powerful men is not entirely true, although that is the impression among many men.

Wealth and power are indeed a strong attraction among some women.

However, women of worthwhile character and worth are more interested in men who show respect and maturity than in material possessions.

It will take maturity to get through the tough times, and honesty will be the strength that will bind the couple together, helping them both stay stronger.

Do not forget that the purpose of a relationship is to provide love, affection, and stability in the family.

Any reasonable man knows that improving himself is a way of developing attractiveness to attract a woman, so in the search for the ideal woman, a man must also ensure that he is the right man.

A natural and healthy feeling in women is that they want to be unique, so they expect to be exceptional in the eyes of a man, which is something a man must understand.

A confident man knows his mind and place in life and stands up for his beliefs.

A man with qualities has natural security, which places him above other men.

Women feel attracted to his masculinity because he gives them the confidence of protection which allows them a relaxing feeling in the relationship.

Real men have the strength of character to be themselves in a changing world because they are always themselves and do not need to participate in fashions or trends to get people to like them.

Instead, these men focus on being the best version of themselves.

This kind of man strives to be better at every stage of life.

Logically this type of man knows how to be successful with women because he knows what women look for in a man.

Women can notice the masculinity and presence of a real man and seek to be known by such a man.

As a fact, most men are suitable for all types of women.

The problem is that some men feel insecure about themselves.

Fortunately, many women are interested in a man's personality rather than his outward appearance.

Although a man needs to care about his physical appearance to make a good impression on a woman, however, many women are not so superficial.

Most women are more interested in a man's behavior and the confidence he inspires in them than in position or appearance.

Therefore, a man with a character knows how to treat a woman well, although today, there may be women who do not feel so attracted more to a man because of it.

As a result, independent women today seek mentally and emotionally strong men to lead in a relationship.

The truth is that a real man knows how to treat a woman well. And such a man knows how to make her feel like a woman.

THE MAN IN THE FAMILY

A man is measured by the depths of his commitments.
-Mark William Goldman

The definition of a successful man will not be entirely accurate if a man has not also succeeded in the sphere of his family.

A complete definition of success includes being a good provider for his family and a teacher and leader. However, unfortunately not all men are aware of this.

Some fathers of families have solved their financial problems; however, they do not control their children, and others have lost control even of their wives.

And it is that being a good provider means more than providing financially.

The family's emotional, physical, and spiritual well-being matters greatly.

There are things that money can't buy.

In the wife's case, providing for her also involves nurturing her self-esteem.

Providing means instills values in the children by caring for the family lifestyle.

As a family leader, a man creates the kind of family he wants, and this is an effort that involves giving one hundred percent of oneself to achieve this goal.

The best way to teach children is through one's behavior, which children, family members, and even the people around us can see.

It is necessary to mention that a good provider is not made overnight.

Instead, this is a process that begins in youth and that, in the future, family happiness will depend on it.

But what is involved in this process of being a good provider? The answer is perhaps contrary to what modern culture teaches.

Although becoming a man may seem distant for a young man, it is not because, in just a few years, a young man will be getting married and becoming a father. For this reason, it is necessary to prepare early.

There is something fundamental that society has forgotten. However, even today, it should be an essential fact that a man should be the primary provider for his immediate family.

In addition, many women would prefer to dedicate themselves to raising their children, even putting economic gains aside to take advantage of more time with their families.

However, for this to be possible, a man must begin to prepare himself from his single years.

One of the first things is to be careful with student loans and credit debts when making large purchases.

Preparing to be a successful future husband and father is best by having a written plan and specifying your financial priorities.

Whether by putting money in a fund for a future family or paying off a student loan.

Whatever you decide to do, you must have a purpose.

Putting your resolutions in writing will help you stay aware of your goals.

Otherwise, you could easily fall into impulse purchases that would sidetrack you from your goals without a plan.

It is good to have fun when you are young, but it is better to have a financial plan, and a mentor can help you choose the best option on how to be successful from the beginning of your economic life.

A mentor can be someone who knows about saving and investing methods and has had financial success.

Typically, young graduates suddenly get their first paycheck and think they need a lot of things, but this is when you must be careful about the temptation to start spending.

To save money as a young man. Instead of moving to a house or a two-bedroom apartment with a nice view, you should share the rent with a roommate since the idea is to save money.

Sharing expenses now instead of leading a lifestyle of freedom is what will provide you financial independence for the future.

Living with a single income when you are married will be possible, but it is necessary that today you do not buy to buy but only when it is necessary.

In married life, your income will help to pay current expenses and the house mortgage.

Your wife's money can be for savings, investments, or emergencies.

If you had debt, at least it would not be increasing more and more but decreasing, which will allow you to continue saving to live debt free and with peace of mind.

Research and mentors talk about the consequences of instant or immediate gratification, a habit that has led many people to a precarious and desperate life over time.

Suppose you have the prudence to take care of your expenses during your youth.

In that case, you could avoid many future problems since important things will arrive in due time and without the pressures and difficulties involved in suddenly trying to obtain them once you are married.

If you are not married yet, it is not a reason not to start saving now because there is nothing like being a good provider for your family.

Even the Bible mentions that: It is more blessed to give than to receive.

Therefore, a good man guides his wife and family skillfully.

However, today the lack of leadership by men in the family is a severe problem.

The reason is that society has forgotten to teach this moral value to young people from the family environment.

Today many men do not realize the seriousness of the problem of not taking leadership in their homes for the family's good.

They do not realize that this failure creates a chain reaction of situations ranging from problems in the spouses to financial problems and problems as parents.

This problem is deeply rooted today because recently, men have lacked this leadership role in their families and while growing up.

Even today, some churches do not teach leadership to men because it goes against modern societal trends.

Selfishness, laziness, lack of ideals, and in other cases, lack of character in husbands are some of the reasons or excuses that make men relegate this responsibility to women.

However, no excuse is an acceptable reason for a man to stop fulfilling his responsibility in the marriage.

Although a man should not have excuses for not fulfilling his role as a family leader, there is something that would move a man to behave as a family leader. It is also something that is or is not there from the beginning of a relationship, and the couple should value this feeling for its great importance, which is love.

This natural feeling is what should guide the family in the spiritual aspect first and in the physical part.

Love is the force that will drive a man to solve communication problems and conflicts in marriage.

It is the feeling that will make the man want to protect and love his wife and family, and it is this feeling that will make a wife fully trust that her husband will faithfully perform his role as a family leader.

When a man acts as the leader of his family, he earns the respect of his wife and children.

And when the family leader makes a mistake but admits his fault, he can still maintain his family's respect.

As a manager runs a business, a leader manages his family and must have extensive knowledge of everything in his house.

Children's discipline, care of the family finances, and the well-being of each house member are the family leader's responsibilities.

Of course, to lead his family spiritually well, the family leader must be a person spiritually committed to his values.

Therefore, the best teaching of values is shown with exemplary behavior and is also where leadership begins.

When a man spends time with his wife and children, he can teach them values, reinforcing the family's unity.

The heart of the family leader must lie anchored in the truth. Otherwise, the man's heart will go carried away by temporary feelings and emotions.

Honesty should be the foundation for every moral decision at home and in daily life.

When a conflict arises with the wife, the husband must be the first to seek reconciliation, as it befits the head of the household.

There is a blessing in being the family leader a man ought to be.

Either way, it is wise to ask for God's guidance to do an excellent job as a leader.

PREPARING TO BE A SUCCESFUL ADULT

Before anything else, preparation is the key to success

— Alexander Graham Bell

There are benefits to being prepared, and a lack of it often leads to disappointment and further loss.

Being prepared is usually synonymous with self-discipline.

Likewise, becoming a well-equipped adult to deal with what life throws at you is better than finding yourself being dragged around aimlessly and trying to navigate difficulties.

Sometimes on a partly cloudy day, people hope it won't rain and decide not to bring an umbrella with them.

Then the rain comes, and they regret not having brought an umbrella, but repenting doesn't help unless experience helps them in the future.

As B Franklin said, you are preparing to fail by failing to get ready.

However, sometimes we live randomly and want to realize our dreams but don't even know how to start.

Regardless of the project, be it a meeting, an interview, a romantic date or to start or end a relationship, an illness, or perhaps the death of a loved one, we are never really prepared to face circumstances.

When we lack preparation, we lose opportunities that sometimes may never come back again.

Life is unpredictable; sometimes, things take us by surprise, so we should have a plan B to act when our circumstances change unexpectedly.

On the other hand, practicing the art of preparation will allow us to get out of difficult and unexpected situations.

Some skills that can help us prepare are our self-discipline and good habits.

We reinforce our self-discipline when we routinely prepare for unexpected situations, taking the necessary time to prepare and putting aside the natural laziness of doing nothing or leaving everything for later.

On the contrary, we avoid excuses by reflecting that what we do is vital for our benefit.

In addition, preparation reinforces strategic thinking because it makes us think about ourselves and all the advantages we will obtain if we have everything we need in advance.

It could be a specific date, perhaps it is a vacation, and everything must be paid and taken care of before leaving home for a particular time.

Maybe pack your luggage, check if you have travel insurance ready, etc.

The higher the difficulty of a task, the higher the level of strategy that we will have to be reasoned.

However, no one is born a master of the required strategic thinking.

But instead, one obtains this ability through practice.

No matter what you are preparing for, you can master this skill.

Although it may seem incredible every time we wake up and get dressed to go somewhere or do an activity, our brain has already devised many strategies to accomplish the tasks appropriately and at the right time.

Although we do not appreciate that our brain has acted strategically to succeed in our daily activities, every thought in our brain is a preparation to hone strategic skills.

The practice of self-discipline and strategic thinking leads to the development of flexibility and mental fluidity.

Flexibility and mental fluidity prepare you to know what others expect from you, make you understand your scope, and be aware that problems may arise at any time.

Therefore, preparation involves envisioning possible scenarios and preparing for different outcomes.

In addition, the habit of being prepared for unforeseen situations develops in the individual the quality of being tenacious, which allows them to stay strong, healthy, and overcome faster after some calamity has occurred.

In general, the habit or discipline of preparation in daily life equips us to take advantage of any opportunity and helps us avoid making the same mistakes.

The main reason for the discipline of preparation in our lives, besides allowing us to take advantage of opportunities, is that when we are young, it can prepare us for adult life.

However, we must implement the art of being prepared in our lives consistently and sustainably.

Among the activities for young people that offer a valuable purpose for the future, we can mention employment and volunteer work, among others. Those activities prepare young people to obtain independence.

Community participation, which includes personal relationships, is also fundamental.

Therefore, reflecting on the preparation to enter adulthood from an early stage is essential.

Good preparation requires planning and education to promote maximum future independence and the ability to make quality decisions.

And the youth stage is the best to start forming good habits that will make adulthood easier.

While the transition to adulthood is taking place, it is possible to learn and grow as a person if you take advantage of the mistakes made up to that moment.

Often the mistakes made during youth are easily forgotten, so we do not take advantage of those first experiences to reflect and learn from them.

The transition from adolescence to adulthood is full of experiences from which we could gain some wisdom.

Supposedly a mature person is wiser than a younger one.

Wisdom would not be an exclusive characteristic of older people if older people didn't learn from mistakes made during youth.

Consequently, we find adults who sadly go from failure to failure when maturity should be different.

A positively developing mind will remove negative self-criticism from its mental environment by changing preconceived ideas and replacing them with more constructive thoughts.

For example, instead of saying or thinking, "I'm not good at doing this or that," one should say, "I know I don't feel capable now, but eventually, I know I will."

It is necessary to recognize and even appreciate our mistakes because we can learn first-hand what we should avoid in the future or how to do something effectively if we learn from our mistakes now.

But this growth in our mental attitude is achieved when we stop making excuses or blaming someone else for our mental negativity.

We all have old and new experiences, which means we can learn all the time and perfect our lives if we want to change and improve.

In childhood, we depended on adults to help us organize our activities and time by telling us what we needed to do and when.

As the transition from childhood to adulthood progresses, we can also begin to schedule all our activities.

As adults, we can organize our time by setting schedules for classes, deadlines, and work.

You can organize your activities using a calendar or a phone app to remember essential things even if you're not in the habit of checking a calendar or keeping an activity log.

Organizing time is effective because you must also focus on rest to recharge your energy.

Having a job as a teenager can help young people foresee in which area, they feel they could develop an eventual professional career.

We can identify our skills and interests and analyze the possibilities of a future market for our ideas when we have our first job.

Though not always the case, once we have the first job, we can think of the education and experience needed to start a business on our own in the future based on what we like or on what we feel comfortable doing in our very first job.

The point is to gain experience from a first job.

While you are young and already have a job, it is time to establish a budget to control expenses, even if you do not yet have the responsibility to pay some bills.

It is vital to start saving money in youth instead of spending it all because saving money is a good start as you enter adulthood.

For past generations, perhaps it was different; however, now, more than in other times, it is vital to be prepared for when the time comes to get married and start another stage in life because the problem is not how much you earn but how much you spend as a young man.

Of course, it is necessary to make regular expenses that are not so vital, like going to concerts, going to the movies, or ordering food, etc.

However, economic experts recommend budgeting between 20 – 30 percent of the total generated for this category of expenses.

But the bottom line is saving for the future, which is the same as being prepared.

Another step toward future financial independence includes building a good credit history, and there are applications where you can explore options about a credit reporter.

It is best to start with a credit card with a credit limit to start building your credit, you can start using your card to make payments that you usually make each month, such as your mobile phone payment, but you must pay the monthly charges in full each month.

Different phone applications offer credit services, such as Nerdwallet, CreditKarma, Wallethub, etc. However, they all provide the same services.

The important thing is the focus on developing a good credit history, which in the future will help you to have at your disposal opportunities to acquire from a car to a house or apartment without any complications or negatives from banks.

Communication skills can be beneficial if you learn them as a young man, and you will need them, especially when you reach adulthood.

The ability to communicate with different people and contexts it is often disregarded.

However, the skill of communication is necessary to participate in activities in your community, for example, by being a member of a church, doing volunteer work in the community, even when looking for the people's approbation on a political campaign.

Talking with different people and in different contexts is something that, as an adult, it is beneficial because good communication is helpful in various circumstances throughout adulthood.

Thinking of saving money, occasionally you can prepare your food.

You can start with something simple as spaghetti!

It is an essential dish that is not so messy to prepare.

You can add sausage, a little beef for protein, and some onions and green peppers to add flavor and variety.

Of course, ham and eggs are a classic for breakfast though it is nothing wrong if you sometimes eat them for dinner.

And as you learn more, you can perfect some dishes until you know how to cook something that you can comfortably enjoy at home.

Even you could pleasantly impress a future wife by inviting her to dinner at home.

A good habit that will help you a lot throughout life is the habit of making your bed every morning.

It does not take time and will make your room look more presentable.

Spending just a few minutes of your time to organize things in the room will prevent creating an uncontrollable mess in which it is impossible to live.

Order never hurt anyone and is one of the best indicators that you are ready to enter adult life.

Also, when you live with a woman, she will thank you for this quality that you have.

In the same way, that order at home is a good habit. It is a good habit to be orderly at work as well.

After working on the company's computer, removing anything you don't want your boss to know about is a good idea.

It is logical to expect that employees check their social networks even at work.

The problem is that someone at work may also be checking how employees use their time during working hours.

If you want to avoid a wrong impression of yourself, maybe it's a good idea to be careful not to post something that gives an undesired impression.

That is why having order in your life as a young man will never be a bad habit.

It is worth mentioning that pursuing our dreams and aspirations is ideal, and in addition, your hobbies help you to reaffirm your self-esteem and give you a feeling of belonging.

As we age, it is more difficult to find people like us who share our same interests.

However, if we search, we will find that we are not alone, and there are always people who share our interests in any matter, either art, sports, or some other kind of work.

One way to feel connected is to get involved in community service, where you can meet other people and probably people with your same interests and help improve conditions in your area.

Engaging in physical activity as a habit for at least an hour a day will provide good health during youth and in adulthood, and exercise will prevent you from gaining weight as the body ages.

Treat everyone with kindness and respect as much as possible because by helping others, you are helping yourself because you never know when you might need help.

Kindness brings happiness and boosts self-esteem by making you feel good about yourself.

Although today it is easy to have many friends through social networks, it is also necessary to have friends in person who can help you at some point.

With whom you can share activities such as going to the movies, a party, or doing some sport, it is good to have friends who share joys, and a friend can provide emotional support when needed.

As you can see, going from youth to adulthood means considering many aspects of life, and continuous learning can lead you to be the best version of yourself.

Everything we learn during youth can help us prepare for optimal and happy adult life.

A life with the woman waiting for the right man, however any man could become the right man for the woman he chooses if he considers that a woman needs someone to lean on as you both move forward towards a fuller adult

IN SEARCH OF HAPPINESS FOR A WOMAN

" I'm tough, ambitious and I know exactly what I want."
-Madonna Ciccone

When comparing past times, it is possible to say that today's women should be the happiest in history because they have more opportunities in any career and greater rights.

Unlike in the past, today, women can choose how many children they want to have or not have children.

Today women don't have to get married to survive, and no one can force them to, and if they get married, they can also ask for a divorce if that's what they want.

However, all this does not seem enough for women to achieve complete happiness.

Fears persist in women that perhaps they are not doing everything right, improving their lives, and doing all the good they seek.

Although modern women enjoy more freedoms than in the past

The truth is that modern women are ten times more prone to depression than they were fifty years ago, and women are twice as likely to fall into depression than their male counterparts.

Paradoxically, in modern society, where many choices abound for women, it does not seem enough to confer happiness to them.

It is undeniable that modern women are proud of all their achievements, privileges, and opportunities that they enjoy today.

Yet, in their struggle for more freedom and social success, most women have lost their sense of happiness.

Today many women would refer to sexual pleasure as what makes them happy, perhaps a nice dinner or a good wine.

Although this type of happiness is rather momentary, permanent happiness is elusive in the lives of most women.

Many books each year struggle to help women find real happiness by discovering their inner selves.

Research projects on the causes of unhappiness in women determined that the lack of meaning in their lives is the leading cause of their lack of happiness.

Many women are inclined to different methods to find happiness.

However, they discover that happiness is still absent in their lives.

Unless they find a perfectly defined idea of happiness, they will continue to live without it.

Research shows that among the things that can offer more lasting happiness is, among others, a sentimental relationship.

Surround yourself with family and friends, be self-employed and independent, have time to carry out activities, and be involved in projects, physical activity, and things that have a spiritual meaning beyond oneself.

Contrary to what personal help literature advises to achieve happiness, what can provide greater satisfaction is the ability to help others.

Understanding the circumstances, a woman goes through in life is vital to knowing how to make her happy.

Although the task of seeking happiness for a woman is not that complicated, it is necessary to have a good understanding of her character and act honestly in dealing with her.

Knowing a woman is knowing her plans, desires, and dreams, and although knowing her is essential, she will not reveal her intimate thoughts to a man.

Instead, it is the man's job to learn to know her and how he must treat her in a relationship, and the woman, in turn, will know how to differentiate the right man from the wrong one.

Finally, men and women are not so different in character and ideals, and they both want the same things in life.

Sometimes it is said that men do not understand women, which is why it would be of great benefit to know what makes women happy or what they expect in a relationship because men are often ignorant about women.

A man would benefit more if, instead of behaving arrogantly, he instead chose to be trustworthy because trustworthiness is something that can make a woman feel safe and comfortable.

Behaving with integrity with the woman you love is essential for a healthy relationship.

Not underestimating little acts of attention with her will remind her of positive things when a minor problem arises between the two.

In the case of any misunderstanding with her, a sincere apology will make her forget the mistake.

As much as possible, a man should dress with style because that pleases a woman, so it is essential to know her tastes, although being oneself should not be ignored completely.

Most women like to talk and be listened to carefully but above all, they want to be understood, and if a man pays attention, he will be able to get to know her better.

Paying attention to a woman when she talks will be rewarded with more understanding between the two.

Since most women want a good man who can be caring and supportive, be that man for her by helping her out to make her life happy.

The main thing is to live a happy life with the woman a man loves.

Understanding her and providing a healthier, more comfortable, and lasting relationship for her by being a committed man is the best way to give a woman true happiness.

And last but never least, fall not into infidelity because such mistake can cause irreparable damage to a relationship.

TO PLEASURE HER

"Most women prefer lovemaking with romance, appreciation, respect, and caring with plenty of foreplay, satisfaction, and afterglow."

— J.F. Kelly

Good sex has to do with good communication. Although usually, women are not as open to expressing their sexual desires as men do.

Women sometimes do not have words to express what they enjoy, and sometimes they do not have enough confidence to comment on what they like in the intimacy.

Although there is a lot of information obtained through research and many comments made by different people from different social levels, the truth is that the best sex is the one that a woman enjoys with whom she feels comfortable and with whom she is happy to do it.

Often investigations and opinions of all kinds of people or experts in the field are unimportant because, after all, it is in the conversation where the couple can express or insinuate what they enjoy most in intimacy.

For instance, a man-woman relationship will work excellently when a man knows how to make a woman feel how special she is to him.

Then they will only need slight hints from each other to know that both are willing to have intimacy when they decide whether they have known each other for a short or a long time.

If you are new to discussing sex with your romantic partner, perhaps you should start with some light flirting which will let a woman know that she is the one you have chosen.

Then you can start expressing yourself more clearly in your conversations with her about the subject of sex.

A man likely feels slightly corny when expressing himself romantically with a woman.

Still, it is time to leave some reservations and start letting her know that she is sexy, basically being a little more direct by letting her know how much you are attracted to her.

You can send a quote through text message to let the woman you love know that you would like to be intimate with her, and she will likely be ready for that encounter after perhaps a romantic dinner.

There's no question that a man should ensure that a woman feels comfortable or safe enough to talk about sex, although slightly risqué messages will generally discourage a woman's interest.

However, every woman wants to feel desired, and these messages always point in the right direction.

A man's message to the woman he loves shows her that she is an essential part of his life.

It is a fact that both men and women know that a healthy sexual relationship will benefit them, and therefore their relationship will become something closer.

Although life is much more than a good sexual relationship, sex is a crucial part of a relationship.

So slight hints of intimacy predispose a woman to the appropriate state of mind.

When you feel comfortable whispering sexy things in your partner's ear, you will see that her levels of passion will rise, which will increase the well-being of the relationship between the both of you.

Therefore, the relationship can be happy and healthy in the bedroom, and consequently, the relationship will become one where sharing things will be more enjoyable. Men are also interested in what a woman likes more, and men enjoy more by knowing that a woman is enjoying more.

When a man understands the emotional language of a woman, it gives him security.

However, the specific issues of a marital relationship and what pleases a woman the most is something that each couple enjoys differently since each couple is also different.

In general, foreplay is something that most couples enjoy practicing.

The specific subjects are something women enjoy and prepare them for body intercourse by increasing their excitement.

It may seem that the statement that the best sexual encounter with a partner begins outside the intimacy of the bedroom does not make sense.

Still, it is in communication through informal coexistence, such as taking a walk with the partner, going to the movies, or having a coffee, when a man predisposes a woman for a possible intimate encounter.

Laid the foundations for sure everything would happen between the couple about sex.

At least in a sincere relationship where the well-being of the woman a man loves is essential, a man will seek to establish robust, honest, and lasting sentimental ties.

Therefore, the foundations for a sexual encounter begin in these circumstances, and a woman can relax and prepare to enjoy the intimate encounter with her partner.

In an environment where no distractions exist, a woman will begin to feel ready to withdraw into the pleasure of the sexual encounter.

In addition to the evident physical differences between men and women, women have different behavioral differences that have more to do with their minds.

Therefore, a man interested in pleasing a woman must understand and accept these differences. Furthermore, although it is not new, a man must remember that sexual pleasure in women has a more profound link with an emotional connection.

When there is an emotional connection in the woman, she can enjoy more the preamble of caresses in her intimate parts that precede the total act of intimacy.

Taking the time to find out what a woman likes in a sexual encounter is essential to making the intimate encounter more pleasurable for her.

Of course, a man must also obtain satisfaction in intimacy with a woman, but he must consider that her satisfaction is a priority.

Understanding that the seduction of women begins not only outside her bedroom but also in their minds then is vital to help her obtain the best sexual pleasure.

So, a man should offer his full attention when he tries to please a woman by caressing her from head to toe.

Caressing a woman's whole body will make her relax, and it will let her know that in such a moment, only she matters.

Foreplay is crucial because, for some women, orgasm is something empty if it doesn't exist a deep connection with her.

Interacting with a woman in an intimate environment is essential to pleasing her.

However, sex alone is not enough to please and make a woman happy, as many different factors complement the sexual union of the couple.

Therefore, pleasing a woman involves both the bedroom and an environment outside.

And, of course, the woman's mind is also involved in the goal of giving her total pleasure and happiness.

So, the ultimate way to please a woman is to love her body and mind in the bedroom.

But a man should also love the character and personality that make her a woman.

MAN, AND HIS FEMALE COUNTERPART

"I would rather trust a woman's instinct than a man's reason."
— Stanley Baldwin

Among the most controversial topics in psychology is the issue of the difference between the sexes, and new approaches to these differences show that they are enormous as far as personality is concerned. So, we cannot ignore those differences.

Differences in the sexes include many aspects ranging from the physical to the psychological.

However, the most significant advances occur in the field of the personality of the sexes, so we must treat these differences more seriously.

The most rejected differences between the sexes are seen from a very narrow level, although this should not be so.

When examining facets of the sexes, recognition is that some characteristics of men allow them to obtain high scores because of certain qualities, and women also score high on other attributes.

These traits seem to indicate that there is not much difference in personality between the sexes when, the differences exist and are very real.

Generally, men and women are not so different in the tendency to obtain gratification from external factors.

Besides, men tend to be more dominant, risky, and less emotional, although many other men do not have these characteristics.

On the other hand, women are more friendly, sensitive, kind, and shy and tend to appreciate the beauty in everything.

Women also focus more on emotions and are more skilled in communication.

Another characteristic of women is that they tend to smile more but cry more often than men.

However, contrary to expectations, the differences between men and women tend to be large, not small.

Regarding the psychological differences between men and women, we can mention that women develop the brain's right hemisphere faster than men, allowing them to speak, pronounce, read earlier, and have a better memory.

Another characteristic of women is that they use both hemispheres of the brain.

Men, on the other hand, develop the Left side faster than women, which allows them to develop the ability to perceive visual information in the environment, better understand mathematics, and solve problems.

Girls are more interested in toys with faces, stuffed animals, and dolls during childhood. And boys are more attracted to blocks and objects that they can manipulate.

Girls tend to talk about things in secret to ensure friendship.

Children talk about activities, what they do and who is the best at activities.

As teenagers, girls often comment on boys and their appearance.

And perhaps the most significant event for girls is to have a boyfriend.

Boys talk more about sports, mechanics, and functions, although they are equally interested in cars and sex.

Somehow logically, when both sexes reach maturity, women are interested in relationships, physical appearance, clothing, and diets. Meanwhile, men talk more about sports, work, money, cars, news, and politics.

Man acquires the feeling of worth through successes that make him feel good about himself, though it is advisable to achieve goals for oneself.

Although, in general, young people as adults continue to be interested in objects more than in people or feelings.

It is not common for men to talk about their problems unless it is to seek expert advice because, for men, it is a sign of weakness to ask for help if they can do it themselves.

The man also has an innate aggressiveness and a sense of territoriality, which is more marked than women.

Also, men's obsession with money is greater than that of women. However, this obsession exposes them to suffering more in situations of financial adversity.

Men often prefer not to ask for advice because they consider it a flaw in their character.

Men use more logic and are more rational, although it is more difficult for them to express their feelings because telling them is the same as feeling threatened, making them withdraw or try to be dominant.

However, men are vulnerable and more dependent on their relationships, and the end of a relationship is devastating for them, but they can also deal better with their anger.

In the case of women, they give more value to love, beauty, and friendship.

Also, women define their sense of worth through the quality of their relationships and feelings.

Also, women often give each other help and moral support.

By socializing and sharing, women experience a sense of worth.

Women also tend to offer selfless help as a show of support.

A characteristic of women is their interest in factors related to physical attractiveness. Therefore, any alteration in the physical beauty aspect is devastating for them, as is the financial part for men.

Undeniably, when men are worried about work or money, women innately interpret it as rejection towards them, which in most cases, their suspicion is unfounded.

However, women tend to be more intuitive and experience a broader range of feelings than men, making men interpret it as a rapid change of emotions.

Therefore, such a change of emotions in women makes it difficult for men to understand women.

Another feminine quality is the sensitivity to sounds and smells, which allows women to emphasize the atmosphere of places.

Fundamental differences in character, personality, and to a lesser degree, cultural differences influence conflicts between men and women.

Among men's most frequent complaints against women is that, according to men, women are always trying to make them change.

Women insist that men never listen, but women often want empathy from their partners.

Men often feel guilty about women's problems and try to give them advice or offer solutions to their problems.

When a woman is angry, it is best not to bother her with questions or talk about anything that requires seriousness, it is best to give her privacy and time, but at another time when she is calm, it will be the appropriate time to chat with her.

Women need love, understanding, respect, and security, and when they are made to feel special and loved, they will be motivated.

On the other hand, man needs something or someone to trust.

A man also needs acceptance, appreciation, approval, and support.

When a man feels needed, it motivates him to act, but a man would hardly express that he sometimes feels incompetent or that he is not good enough for something.

The man needs independence and position.

On the other hand, a woman has a greater need for intimacy and association.

There are other significant differences between men and women. Still, none of these differences make one sex better than the other because these differences denote precisely that both are just different.

Therefore, both sexes are undeniably essential and do not need any change; instead, their differences are their essence that makes them unique.

Observations on the differences between the sexes help us to understand a little about the complexity of each one.

Therefore, the information allows us to understand both sexes and their personalities.

Understanding and accepting the differences between the sexes is vital to a healthy coexistence and improving attitude and compassion when relating to the opposite sex.

It is imperative not to forget that kindness, interest, and respect will be the keys to achieving a better relationship in the future or an existing one.

BASICS OF A HEALTHY RELATIONSHIP

A healthy relationship keeps the doors and windows wide open. Plenty of air is circulating and no one feels trapped. Relationships thrive in this environment. Keep your doors and windows open. If the person is meant to be in your life, all the open doors and windows in the world, will not make them leave. Trust the truth.

— Unknown

Relationships as a couple contribute to our greatest joys but also our greatest heartaches (in the romantic sense)

But in other words, relationships are challenging to maintain without causing us some suffering when they go wrong, and we feel confused and sorry.

We have all been in situations of preoccupation because of a relationship.

And almost no one has been exempted from it.

The reality is that there are no perfect relationships.

Whether because of children, parents, or spouses, all of us have experienced problems in our relationships.

Sometimes problems derive from a lack of understanding or another cause, at least for some time.

Although we know that if we are willing to offer kindness, humility, and respect and keep our lines of communication open and get the same from the other party, we can experience a deep connection, love, acceptance, and peace of mind.

Most people struggle to maintain healthy and happy relationships even though the environment in which we live often promotes superficial values that cause us to be confused about what is healthy and of importance.

Of course, not all situations in relationships are the same. However, some elements can help us promote general well-being to live our relationships in healthy and satisfactory ways.

Initially, we feel attracted to someone for various reasons such as their physical appearance, personality, and emotional first date, we are captivated by the idea of being in front of that person, and we love the first feelings.

As we move forward in the relationship and because of those first feelings, we refuse to meditate on the elementary fundamentals that can create a healthy relationship that can prosper our relationship.

Although every relationship can be unforgettable in its beginnings, we must not forget that a relationship is much more than feeling good in it.

Just as maintaining a machine is essential, love also needs attention to survive.

Eventually, the feeling of love gives the impression of diminishing however it does not mean that love is disappearing.

According to relationship counselors, falling in love is easy, but it is the maintaining of love that takes effort.

So, whether you've been in a relationship in the past or a first relationship, it's important to consider the essential elements that can create and maintain a healthy relationship.

Let us consider the following qualities we need to stimulate to develop and live a successful and pleasant relationship.

Listening and valuing the opinion of each one in the relationship and trying to understand the other's point of view, even if one disagrees with the other's perspective, will prevent misunderstandings.

The wisest attitude towards each other's goals is to

seek to be of help and support for the ideas or ambitions of the other party.

In a relationship, both should be able to share their dreams and ideals without fear of negative criticism; instead, one would expect to receive support and understanding even if one of the two is not very interested in the goals of the other.

There should be a good level of understanding in the relationship. Therefore, the essentials are honesty and respect between the two since these factors are essential because they can create an atmosphere of certainty and affection.

Are we able to admit when we have been wrong?

The truth is that nobody likes to admit that they were wrong and when the time comes when we realize that all this time our partner has been correct and we were wrong, it is frustrating, but what remains is to ask for an apology and accept our mistake.

After all, accepting our mistakes before our partner is what ultimately will strengthen the relationship.

Respect is fundamental in any relationship because it generates trust, security, and well-being.

However, this consideration does not have to come on its own. Instead, it is something we can also learn.

Respect is not just about respecting your partner but also their friends, family, and any activities your partner does or practices.

There is an understated but effective way to enjoy a better and a healthy relationship with your partner: the ability to make each other laugh.

Some say that one cannot genuinely love another person if that person does not laugh with us, but it makes sense since people who can laugh together create stronger bonds of affection.

Also, people who laugh together have more advantages when overcoming conflicts.

There are men who, thanks to their ability to make a woman smile, can win her affections faster than anyone else.

Smiling with the partner adds happiness and growth to the relationship.

Understanding the need for space means recognizing that spending time apart from each other is a healthy habit because it balances the time a couple spends together and apart.

Occasionally spending time apart is healthy for a relationship because that time helps maintain each other's individuality.

Being alone also promotes meditating on our emotions and needs and allows us to have clarity of mind from which both in the relationship can benefit.

Because everyone is different, differences of opinion will lead to disagreements in a relationship.

However, a couple can happily co-exist even when each has a different perspective or other preference.

Having differences does not mean that a relationship is not healthy, but very often, condescension in the relationship is necessary to resolve a conflict.

It is natural to have disagreements, but a couple can resolve conflicts with communication and respect.

Usually, the couple continuously learns something in the process and strengthens the relationship.

In a relationship, both parties are equal and should treat each other fairly. After all, they are a team and should support each other.

Equality in the relationship means that one partner must respect the interests of the other to a reasonable level, which is the opposite of one party in the relationship being the dominant one.

Therefore, as a team, a couple must fight for the same goals.

The appreciation of one towards the other is of great importance where not much is required.

Sometimes a simple thank you addressed to the spouse is enough to help brighten their day.

Appreciation is fundamental, as it can make both in the relationship feel good about themselves to continue their lives as a couple with new vigor.

REBUILDING THE TRUST AFTER THE DAMAGE DONE

Never leave a true relationship for a few faults, nobody is perfect, nobody is correct, in the end affection is always greater than perfection.

-Unknown

The faith of putting our trust in a person and knowing that said person will not cause us any harm since his honesty makes them someone honorably and reliable towards ourselves is what we call trust.

And as known trust is the foundation of any relationship. Still, unfortunately, that trust can also be broken by any of the individuals that make up the relationship.

Often the failure is due to infidelity, and it can also be the result of one party betraying the other's sense of security and trust in the relationship.

However, whatever the cause of this betrayal of trust is, the hope is that not everything is lost.

And when trying to restore broken trust in a marriage or dating relationship, the steps to regain the confidence of the hurt person are invariably the same in each case.

When there is a common goal of rebuilding a marriage, first and foremost, there must be the desire to restore the relationship on both sides of the relationship.

The process of rebuilding trust in a marriage is always a two-way affair where the couple is willing to work together.

However, when the offended spouse does not want reconciliation because the wound is profound, in such a case, reconciliation is not possible.

In rebuilding a relationship, both parties must be honest and willing to work and do whatever it takes to make the relationship work again, as this process is not a one-sided project.

Reconciliation requires that both parties give of themselves.

When the couple is willing to save their relationship and regain trust, reconciliation is possible, and a relationship can even become stronger and prosperous.

A couple can restore trust, but to bring about the repairing of faith is necessary that parties involved be willing to put effort into trying to alleviate and ultimately be willing to forgive and forget this injury to the relationship.

Since a relationship involves two people, rebuilding a relationship depends on both parties being willing to reestablish it.

Therefore, the person who has suffered the betrayal must be willing to forgive.

The couple in these circumstances must be interested in taking the first steps toward repairing the lost trust, and both must be willing to put efforts into rebuilding their relationship.

However, the willingness to apologize will not be enough without a sincere and honest desire to rebuild the relationship.

Keeping the lines of communication open during reconciliation can create a more transparent relationship in the couple and a more sincere closeness.

And during this reconciliation process, it is an excellent time to open about the harm that has been caused to the loved one or to whoever it is with whom one has broken their trust.

Admitting guilt is the right way when seeking

forgiveness.

It is better to recognize the wrongdoing rather than wait until someone else says it for us.

The search for forgiveness must be honest, trying to heal the relationship by speaking from the heart.

In no way should one look to blame others for the wrong behavior that one has done, as this could only cause more division instead of fixing the relationship.

In a reconciliation, there is a desire to get ahead in the relationship.

Then conversation must be with honesty and affection towards the other.

The offending party must show that they are genuinely sorry for acting irresponsibly.

If a person who has betrayed a spouse's trust does not feel genuinely remorseful, perhaps they need to examine themselves about the acts committed and how they have seriously affected others.

To understand a hurt person, you must try to put yourself in their place and know how it feels when someone breaks your trust.

The person who has betrayed someone's trust in this way should have the courage to show remorse through a sincere and thoughtful apology, expressing sorrow for those actions and wishing from the inside never to commit such act again.

When trying to rebuild a relationship, direct actions must make the new compromise instead of making word promises.

There is an effective way to regain trust when rebuilding a relationship, and now words are not enough, but actions.

When trying to repair the damage in the relationship, there will be reactions on the part of the hurt person, and the response will depend on the extent of the damage caused.

Logically there can be tears, screams, and offenses towards the unfaithful party.

However, the offensive party may expect such a reaction, but it will be prudent to respond to these emotions with empathy and understanding to avoid making things worse.

Instead, the offender should remain calm and try to reassure the other person in the most positive way possible, knowing that the claims will eventually end.

When the offender is not entirely willing to save the relationship and hides the truth, that attitude will be equally damaging to the relationship.

Not admitting guilt will prevent the relationship from being restored.

But when the offending party truly wants to save the relationship, speaking honestly and considerately will be the foundation for moving forward in rebuilding a relationship.

Opening emotionally and committing to healing the relationship is the first step, and the second is paying attention to the hurt person's thoughts and emotions.

Remember that the person who has suffered the deception needs to get the things that hurt off their chest.

Listen carefully to a heart that wishes to show the damage suffered with a genuine desire not to hurt that person again but to show the firm wants to help heal by listening with empathy to the injured person.

It is possible that for a long time, the person who committed the fault will have to continue apologizing and this will depend on the degree of pain caused to the injured person.

However, listening with empathy will allow you to move forward in the healing process.

Meanwhile, the offending party can take advantage of this time for examination by asking himself what the cause of having betrayed the spouse's trust is.

The offender should examine himself, avoiding blaming third parties.

Trying to understand the causes from within yourself and examining your fears and frustrations will most likely help you find answers.

If the deception was perhaps due to feelings of abandonment or some other cause, in any case, seeking counsel is likely to be needed.

In the healing process, practicing regular conversations with purpose is best.

Once the emotions have calmed down, and the anger or resentment has subsided, it is time for the party that suffered the most damage to be willing to sit down and listen to the reasons that led the spouse or partner to have done the damage to the relationship that held them together.

Again, it is not appropriate to want to blame the victim of the deception.

Instead, use everything learned and meditate to advance in the relationship through conversations with the purpose of healing and forgetting.

When there is affection, both parties will want to help continue through whatever fear or emotional difficulty has been the cause of the problem.

The goal of talking is to identify the true causes and face the emotions so that the wounds in the relationship can soon heal.

Another step towards repairing the relationship is showing transparency in all forms, which will help the spouse regain trust.

Total transparency is vital for recovery; however, recovery will be difficult if the offender continues hiding something.

When the relationship is valued, there will be a willingness to be transparent with the desire that the hurt person can see the offender's interest in rebuilding the lost trust and saving the relationship.

Unfortunately, in cases where the cheating spouse is unwilling to support rebuilding the marriage, then the course of action must be to go ahead on their own.

The truth is many couples continue together for years despite the infidelity of one of the parties, which never accepts guilt for their behavior.

However, this type of relationship can never be the same again.

In these cases, there will always be a lack of true intimacy after destroying the trust that once existed.

However, some persons can forgive in their hearts for another person's harmful behavior even though there was never any apology.

This type of person can continue without resentment and pain, which allows them to let go of the burden of resentment without waiting for an apology.

Not many people can ignore an offense like betraying you; however, the truth is that you do yourself a favor when you forgive.

In forgiving, you eliminate the burden of feelings and resentments that came to you because of someone who broke your trust.

For your well-being, reflecting on the best attitude after suffering a deception in the relationship is necessary.

When the affection of a hurt person persists, it is an excellent option to consider forgiveness because when you can forgive, you can leave the wound behind.

Forgiving is healthy for you physically and emotionally because forgiving and forgetting are some of the most beneficial forms of moving forward in a relationship.

Sometimes a wound can be so great that it is impossible to continue with a relationship. However, in some cases, forgiveness can still be a good option.

It can be that old hurts, disappointments, betrayals, and resentment waste your time and energy, and pain held for too long can eventually turn into bitterness.

On the contrary, the quality of forgiveness helps a person reduce the risk of cardiovascular problems, lowers cholesterol levels, improves sleep quality, reduces blood pressure, and helps with anxiety and depression, among other factors harmful to people's health.

Sometimes the person who committed the offense finds it easy to adopt the attitude of being on the defensive.

A defensive attitude does not improve the repair of the damage in the relationship and, on the contrary, only aggravates it.

The form of apology is not as important as the fact that the apology must be a genuine desire to repair the relationship.

Repairing a relationship requires reestablishing trust, so both parties must find the time to reflect and understand the causes that led to that situation.

Then, searching for solutions to survive the cheating crisis, the couple could try to create new positive experiences together.

If optimism still exists in both, it is possible to go through the problem.

Creating new happy moments together can reestablish a connection positively.

After someone has betrayed our trust, we tend to assume that no one is honest, even our friends.

However, we must avoid this kind of reasoning, or we could fall into a spiral of negativity.

In circumstances of mistrust, it would be best to consider our relationships with family, close friends, and others we know to realize that not all people are interested in harming others.

The reality is that, just as there are dishonest people, there are also honest people. And we must know how to distinguish between the two.

When trying to rebuild a relationship, seeking good and honest communication with the spouse is of vital importance.

Also, the offended party should try to let the other know what would help them to be able to trust again or what would make them feel supported and safe again, and they should express their needs in a straightforward way to the other.

Feeling vulnerable is not always harmful in relationships because when you stop being defensive, you can put the rapprochement aside, allowing intimate moments that favor restoring the damaged relationship.

Although not an ideal example, a damaged relationship can be an opportunity to start fresh, looking to fan the flame of a new beginning between the two in the relationship.

The language of love can always make a couple aware of offering the other what it takes to feel loved and supported.

Where there is communication, there is hope.

When a couple forgets the past and its mistakes, they can look to the future.

When a couple can regain trust, they are ready for a new beginning.

Maintaining communication with your partner is always essential to rebuilding or starting, and it is even more important to keep active communication in an existing relationship.

As absurd as it may seem, sometimes infidelity may not be among an offender's plans.

However, it is also true that pride and caprice are extreme in some people, which people fight against within themselves. Still, now it is about making the best decision in the search for solutions to continue with a special relationship you do not want to lose.

Relationships in which the ties have been deep need forgiveness because, unfortunately, everyone makes mistakes.

We all need forgiveness, and we all need to be able to forgive.

Sometimes it is most necessary when a person is genuinely sorry for his mistake and wishes to amend his relationship or marriage.

Even more when the hurt person still finds something of value in the defrauder and still wants to forgive.

Something not always considered by couples is that there is not a perfect relationship and that, over time, no relationship can survive without forgiving some wrong behavior.

However, something is apparent forgiveness does not mean absolution.

Forgiveness is the decision to forget resentment to move on, and although forgiving can be very difficult, it is essential if a relationship is to continue.

CONSIDERATIONS TO ENJOY A STRONG RELATIONSHIP

"Sometimes two people have to fall apart to realize how much they need to fall back together."

— Colleen Hoover

Someone has said that what separates love from hate is a fine line.

Unfortunately, this statement is true because the reality is that relationships are often fragile and can be affected by tiny things if they don't get the necessary care and attention.

Usually, different stages form a relationship that goes from courtship to marriage.

And throughout this process, couples invariably go through small and big obstacles.

Relationships need true love and affection to survive all the hurdles they encounter.

But the biggest obstacle a couple must overcome is the tiredness one of the two members usually starts to feel at certain stages in the relationship and is here when a couple needs to start working harder as a team.

Because nothing is forever, a honeymoon also ends, and a couple enters a new relationship phase where both begin to feel comfortable being themselves.

However, feeling too comfortable in a relationship, be it marriage or dating, can be detrimental to a relationship.

Often it doesn't take something drastic to happen to the couple to ruin the relationship.

Sometimes are many small things that can cause significant damage in a relationship.

There are reasons why a couple breaks up, and ironically most of the reasons that cause the separation could be prevented if only the couple had the will to look for and understand the causes of the problems in the first place.

Some signs that show something is not right are apparent.

Still, others come in subtle forms of negativity that tend to accumulate over time until, like an overflowing dam, they explode and can break the strongest bonds sustaining the unity of a couple.

Couples expect their love will last forever.

However, if a couple does not know how to navigate through all the obstacles they will find on their way, they can crash against adversities and then disappear into nothing.

So, it is vital to know how to maneuver the relationship away from dangers.

When a couple knows how to work as a team and cross the danger zones, a relationship can survive, strengthen, and grow.

The truth is, romantic love is more than honey on flakes on Valentine's Day,

True love needs an environment of honesty and effort to grow happy and healthy and, above all, good habits from the two in the relationship.

The reason to consider the things that are not so beneficial to a relationship and avoid them is to be fully equipped with the necessary knowledge to enjoy a long-lasting and fulfilling relationship.

One of the things to know is to never take the partner for granted.

Just as a dish that should be delicious, if there is no care in its preparation, it can become unpleasant to the taste.

The same thing happens with relationships if they don't get adequate attention and care.

In marriage, priorities often change, and attending to the partner's needs is essential, just like at the beginning of the relationship.

You should also continue to appreciate the qualities that initially made you fall in love with your partner.

Both in the relationship must continue over time to demonstrate their love and appreciation for each other.

Another factor that significantly damages a relationship is holding grudges, which can hinder maintaining a healthy relationship.

Therefore, genuine forgiveness is essential for a couple to continue in an optimal marriage.

Accepting that we all make mistakes shows maturity, but if we cannot get this truth, we won't be able to be completely happy in life.

When there is a tendency to harbor negative emotions, coexistence and understanding become problematic, and achieving complete happiness will be just a beautiful dream.

The reality is that no relationship is easy, and even the most in-love couple will encounter unfortunate sad moments.

Resentment: Resentment also brings jealousy and bitterness to life.

However, to avoid harmful feelings, it is better to talk with your partner about what bothers them so that you can enjoy a happy and healthy connection with your spouse.

In couples, the moment of calm generally returns after an argument.

However, it is advisable not to forget but to analyze together what caused the fight.

When the reason for a problem is not analyzed, either one of the two could retain resentments that little by little accumulate until they explode in one of the two.

Taking for granted: A tendency that exists in people is to put their own needs first; however, if such tendency continues in marriage, it will be detrimental to the proper functioning of the relationship.

A hallmark of any successful relationship is care and attention to each other's needs; commitment and collaboration can make a relationship work.

Doubts: On the other hand, when someone harbors doubt about their partner, such a relationship will hardly prosper since trust is an essential quality in a couple's life.

We could say that without trust, all attempts to maintain a relationship will be in vain since doubt can only create an emptiness.

Insecurity in couples can lead to terrible disasters when they do nothing to correct those flaws.

When a person keeps feelings of low esteem either as a lover or spouse in marriage, there is a risk of falling into harmful behaviors that usually trigger the breakup of a relationship.

The solution to insecurity is to build self-confidence and faith in everyone's qualities.

Blame: Blaming the partner is one of the most harmful attitudes in a couple because such behavior can spoil what could well be a beautiful relationship.

Instead of the practice of blaming someone else, it would be best to learn to say I'm sorry when one in the couple made a mistake.

Making someone responsible for big or small mistakes is not recommended because it directly impacts and destroys the pleasant moments and feelings that the couple had.

The coexistence of the couple should not be a competition, so ignoring some minor mistake does not harm anyone.

And although no one expects misunderstandings or sad moments in a relationship, unfortunately, even the most loving couples have arguments.

When a problem arises in the couple, it does not mean that we should lose our temper.

On the contrary, even in unfortunate moments, we should show kindness and try to understand the spouse or girlfriend to avoid unfairly damaging a good relationship.

Too much depending : Often people forget to be themselves, and sometimes a couple forgets that they are also people with different characteristics.

In the process of daily life, they become each other's life.

However, you must know that a couple also needs their own life concerning the other.

Forgetting to retain individuality in a couple's life could end depending excessively on the other.

In addition to the fact that it might not always be possible to have the support of the other, many dependencies can suffocate anyone in the long run.

Being ignorant about appearance: Maybe it is hard to believe, but the level of pride you reflect in your appearance speaks volumes about your values and how much or little you value your relationship.

When someone downplays their appearance, they show not only their lack of care but also their lack of self-improvement, which indicates their level of interest in the relationship.

In the long run, neglect of personal appearance will negatively impact the quality of the relationship, mainly when the other party is motivated by a good presentation.

Therefore, you're mistaken if you mistakenly believe that your partner is not interested in the impression you make on others.

It is advisable not to neglect personal grooming because it could be a severe failure.

Disrespect: Being respectful to a woman in a relationship will hardly ever cause problems.

On the contrary, disrespecting each other in a relationship could be the reason to end it.

Usually, the foundation of a good relationship is respecting each other in any circumstance.

Regarding the couple, respect becomes a bond that strengthens any relationship, especially between spouses.

Being overly possessive: It is understandable that in a relationship, sometimes there is a fear of losing the love of the spouse or partner.

The fear of losing someone's love makes at least one of the members in the relationship behave insecurely towards their partner.

However, that does not mean one should act overly possessively towards the other person.

To a certain degree, jealousy is a good emotion in the couple, but when jealousy is excessive, it can suffocate the other person.

It happens that the greater the jealousy towards a person, the greater the need to escape from a relationship with said person.

Therefore, couples should be careful about excessive jealousy.

Experiencing a constant bad mood due to jealousy signifies that this emotion has reached a negative point and could affect the relationship.

Jealousy often has no factual basis and is only fueled by imaginary scenarios, so it would be wise to reflect and think about how to solve this problem by talking with your partner.

Not allowing each other space: Some couples can share almost everything, but there are others for whom their things and their own space are essential and exclusive. When privacy is not respected, a healthy relationship will not be possible.

You cannot impose your own will on the couple's will; therefore, respecting the other's space is essential, and if you don't, you risk losing the other person.

It is not good to depend too much on the other person.

That is why it is healthy to have friends with whom to distract yourself from time to time and allow the couple their own space to avoid problems.

A close-knit relationship is beautiful and healthy because there is company and support. Still, a couple must also have space to breathe because, overall, a relationship with a degree of freedom produces closeness.

Mistreating: Something that spouses must always avoid is some abuse in front of family or friends because it speaks very poorly of oneself and is a severe fault in a relationship.

Although some believe that the spouse is their property, that belief is not wise.

That behavior negatively affects the mood and self-esteem of a person and, in the long run, ruins the emotional stability of the spouse and can cause the end of the relationship.

Infidelity: Someone has said that the first look is free, and a little flirtation can be usual to some extent.

But no one can tolerate infidelity.

Cheating on your partner can create a big problem with severe consequences and trying to hide it is not even beneficial for the perpetrator.

When the time comes when the couple finds out about the affair, everything can get out of order.

The most advisable thing is to be faithful to the couple, and if there is something against the spouse, it is best to talk about it in time.

Being involved in infidelity outside the marriage could be the end and the beginning of many difficulties.

Gap in communication: Pride and lack of communication can cause the same damage in a couple's relationship.

An ample space of time without talking can be a reason for misunderstandings and even be the reason for the end of a relationship.

It is essential to ask your spouse how a day has been and tell how yours has been too, because talking to each other forms a healthy and robust relationship and talking also allows people to relax the feeling of boredom.

Good communication with loved ones often acts like medicine for the mind.

In the end, a couple should be confident to express their feelings and concerns without fearing that expressing themselves will cause arguments.

So, there should be no fear of discussing doubts in the heart because we must remember that communication is the key to properly functioning in any relationship.

Failing to make time for each other: For a relationship to progress optimally, both must contribute their time, attention, and effort without affecting the needs of each other.

Making time to dedicate to a loved one promotes the union of the two and is the best incentive to continue together.

The emotional need to feel a hug or kiss and be there in someone's life makes people feel special and loved in a relationship.

Saying 'I love you': Something that will never be excessive in a strong relationship is often saying "I love you" to the loved one.

In daily life, couples sometimes forget to express their feelings to each other but neglecting that detail can weaken their bond.

It is a mistake to think that the phrase 'I love you ' is only necessary at the beginning of a relationship.

Letting the spouse know you love them can reenergize life together and create a sense of happiness.

Issues on physical contact: A couple's relationship could end if one of the two has problems enjoying intimacy.

When there is a sexual problem in the couple, it is best to seek professional help and not blame each other.

First, the spouses need to find an adequate solution because when there is no good intimacy, a relationship may not last.

Intimacy is the fundamental connection between man and woman. It is also the most genuine physical and emotional connection and is a vital and indispensable aspect that unites two people.

When a couple has problems reaching this point in coexistence, there is no genuine relationship between the two.

However, intimacy is much more than the superficial knowledge of a person's body.

Intimacy also means that a person truly knows another, and both share a bond of trust, understanding, and commitment.

There may also be a physical connection if there is an emotional connection. Still, if physical contact is not present, it will be a big problem for various reasons related to multiple causes.

The most common causes of lack of physical contact can be a lack of communication, depression, anxiety, or mental problems.

To solve sex problems in the couple, both need to be more open, honest, considerate, and avoid judging each other.

Although we live in a very sexualized society, many people are dissatisfied with their sexual lives and ignore how to solve their problems.

Sexual desire varies significantly from one person to another and varies due to circumstances in a particular period.

Desire can be aroused through imagination, fantasies, or perceiving a person one finds attractive.

Sexual desire can change from a positively intense degree to being neutral or intensely negative.

Although in people, it is standard for levels of desire to rise or fall at different times of life.

The point is that when the physical relationship is a problem, it is possible to analyze the situation and find a solution to restore the relationship.

Sometimes talking is the best solution, but keep in mind that communication must be from both sides and that it is about talking and listening between the couple.

A couple can feel more united when there are few conflicts, arguments, or heated disagreements between them.

The willingness to calmly handle their anger or frustration helps them quickly restore intimacy.

When the couple performs activities that they both enjoy together, they can create more closeness for intimacy.

To strengthen their intimate relationship, sometimes, the couple should accept counseling from a professional to better resolve any conflict that may affect their relationship.

Excessive whining : If there are constant complaints for one reason or another by one of the spouses in the relationship, coexistence becomes unbearable.

No one likes having to deal with someone in a constant bad mood.

Of course, not everything in life can be happy moments.

However, one should not complain about everything in life.

Instead, life is like a mixture of sour and sweet and accepting life as it is that is living.

Complaining is typical in people, but in romantic situations, it is not advisable to downplay this behavior in any of the members that make up the relationship.

Sometimes constant complaining is like a strategy to show the spouse's disagreement with something.

Although in excess, this behavior can cause a lot of damage.

Sometimes the person complaining is just seeking attention in one or more areas of the relationship, but whatever the exact cause is, it is best to talk about it.

Being romantic: A bit of romanticism must not disappear in a relationship because it shows affection in the couple and makes the union work better.

Moreover, showing a bit of romance is not a difficult job at all.

Simple details such as a romantic dinner, having coffee together, or dressing up in a particular form for the spouse can work wonders in marital life.

Romantic relationships also need maintenance, the same as all things in life.

To rekindle the fire of love in a relationship, details like sending small notes of loving affection are necessary.

Maybe a gift or flowers on a particular day, and knowing the spouse's preferences, such as their favorite food or place.

Also, listening when they have something to say and showing them physical affection, such as kisses, and hugs, among other forms, can strengthen a relationship.

In a love relationship, the details always work for the couple.

Bottom line is: Not neglecting details and attention in a couple's life or dating relationship is crucial since togetherness depends on it.

The little things are sometimes overlooked but are actually very important.

Giving proper attention to details in the relationship can make the couple's coexistence like paradise on earth.

However, being able to love someone is possible only when one can love oneself first.

Giving all of yourself to someone may not be true love, and you must have the ability to have a life outside of the love relationship, or you run the risk of not being able to perceive yourself truly.

The reason to love yourself is that by doing so, your life can be rich in mental health, opportunity, and the chance to be happy in a relationship

REASONS TO BE IN A RELATIONSHIP

"Love has nothing to do with what you are expecting to get—only with what you are expecting to give—which is everything."

—Katharine Hepburn

Love is a unique feeling, perhaps impossible to describe in magnitude and logic.

It is also different and unique for each person.

Only a minority in the world could say that they do not know it, but the most significant thing about love is that everybody wants it to be in their lives because it has a purpose, which is always happiness.

The love between a man and a woman is undoubtedly the most remarkable thing in this life.

When there is love, we learn to share, grow, and love ourselves and others.

When a man and a woman are united in marriage, they can perfect the feeling of love towards themselves and the world in which they live.

By being in a relationship, the couple can provide each other with emotional and financial support, a sense of security, and an abundance of affection.

Loneliness is practically non-existent thanks to the love in a couple; even the fun in them is excellent.

The ability to procreate a family makes the love of a couple the basis of life.

And the union of man and woman is also a safer and healthier environment for sexual needs, and the commitment between the two can provide many vital things in addition to intimacy.

Also, the union offers them passion, joy, satisfaction, and comfort, among many other things necessary for life.

THE END